The Hitch-hiker
and Other Short Stories

CW00552332

« Lire en anglais »

BRADBURY *Ray*
Kaleidoscope and
   Other Short Stories
The Martian Chronicles
   A Story of Love
   and Other
   Non-Science
   Fiction Stories
The Last Circus.
   Stories and
   Interwievs

CAPOTE *Truman*
Breakfast at Tiffany's
Handcarved Coffins

DAHL *Roald*
Someone Like You
   and Other Short
   Stories
The Hitch-hiker and
   Other Short Stories
Mr Botibol and Other
   Short Stories

FAULKNER *William*
Stories of New Orleans

FITZGERALD *F. Scott*
Pat Hobby and Orson
   Welles and Other
   Short Stories

GREENE *Graham*
The Basement Room
   and Other Short
   Stories
The Third Man

HAMMETT *Dashiell-*
CHANDLER *Raymond*
American Detective
Stories of Today

HEMINGWAY *Ernest*
The Killers and Other
   Short Stories
The Old Man and the
   Sea

HIGHSMITH *Patricia*
Please don't Shoot
   the Trees
Trouble at the Jade
   Towers and Other
   Short Stories

JOYCE *James*
Dubliners

MAUGHAM *Somerset*
The Escape and Other
   Short Stories
The Flip of a Coin
   and Other Short
   Stories

SAKI
The Seven Cream
   Jugs and Other Short
   Stories
The Open Window
   and Other Short
   Stories

SHAKESPEARE
Hamlet

STEINBECK *John*
The Snake and Other
Short Stories

UHLMAN *Fred*
Reunion (L'Ami
retrouvé)

———

Nine English Short
Stories
Seven American Short
Stories
The American Press
of Today
A Long Spoon and
Other Short Stories
Simple Arithmetic and
Other American Short
Stories
Thirteen Modern
English and American
Short Stories
English Ghost Stories
English Crime Stories
of Today
The British Press

———

*Premières lectures en
anglais :*
The Umbrella Man
and Other Short
Stories

Bilingues

Des œuvres de S. Bollow, E. Caldwell, L. Carroll, G.K. Chesterton,
J. Conrad, A. Conan Doyle, E.H. Forster, G. Greene, T. Hardy, A. Huxley,
J. Joyce, R. Kipling, J. London, K. Mansfield, H. Melville, O.Henry,
E. Poe, A. Sillitoe, R.L. Stevenson, J. Swift, M. Twain, H.G. Wells,
O. Wilde, V. Woolf, des recueils thématiques de nouvelles.

LIRE EN ANGLAIS
Collection dirigée par Henri Yvinec

Roald Dahl

The Hitch-hiker
and Other Short Stories

Choix et annotations par Chantal Yvinec
Professeur d'anglais

Le Livre de Poche

Abbreviations

Am.: American
cf.: confer (see)
excl.: exclamation
fam.: familiar or informal
pl.: plural
sb.: somebody
sing.: singular
sl.: slang
sth.: something

La collection "Les Langues Modernes" n'a pas de lien avec l'A.P.L.V. et les ouvrages qu'elle publie le sont sous sa seule responsabilité.

©Roald Dahl 1977 *(The Hitch-hiker)*,
1945 *(Death of An Old Man)*,
1951 *(Taste)*,
1954 *(The Way Up To Heaven)*,
1952 *(Dip in the Pool)*

© Librairie Générale Française, 1989, pour la présentation et les notes.

Sommaire

Tout naturellement, après quelques années d'étude d'une langue étrangère, naît l'envie de découvrir sa littérature. Mais, par ailleurs, le vocabulaire dont on dispose est souvent insuffisant. La perspective de recherches lexicales multipliées chez le lecteur isolé, la présentation fastidieuse du vocabulaire, pour le professeur, sont autant d'obstacles redoutables. C'est pour tenter de les aplanir que nous proposons cette nouvelle collection.

Celle-ci constitue une étape vers la lecture autonome, sans dictionnaire ni traduction, grâce à des notes facilement repérables. S'agissant des élèves de lycée, les ouvrages de cette collection seront un précieux instrument pédagogique pour les enseignants en langues étrangères puisque les recommandations pédagogiques officielles (Bulletin officiel de l'Éducation nationale du 9 juillet 1987) les invitent à "faire de l'entraînement à la lecture individuelle une activité régulière" qui pourra aller jusqu'à une heure hebdomadaire. Ces recueils de textes devraient ainsi servir de complément à l'étude de la civilisation.

Le lecteur trouvera donc :

En page de gauche

Des textes contemporains choisis pour leur intérêt littéraire et la qualité de leur langue.

En page de droite

Des notes juxtalinéaires rédigées dans la langue du texte, qui aident le lecteur à

Comprendre

Tous les mots et expressions difficiles contenus dans la ligne

9

de gauche sont reproduits en caractères gras et expliqués dans le contexte.

Observer

Des notes d'observation de la langue soulignent le caractère idiomatique de certaines tournures ou constructions.

Apprendre

Dans un but d'enrichissement lexical, certaines notes proposent enfin des synonymes, des antonymes, des expressions faisant appel aux mots qui figurent dans le texte.

Grammaire au fil des nouvelles

Chaque nouvelle est suivie de phrases de thème inspirées du texte avec références à celui-ci pour le corrigé. En les traduisant le lecteur, mis sur la voie par des italiques et/ou des amorces d'explication, révise les structures rebelles les plus courantes ; cette petite "grammaire en contexte" est fondée sur la fréquence des erreurs.

Vocabulaire

En fin de volume une liste d'un millier de mots contenus dans les nouvelles, suivis de leur traduction, comporte, entre autres, les verbes irréguliers et les mots qui n'ont pas été annotés faute de place ou parce que leur sens était évident dans le contexte. Grâce à ce lexique on pourra, en dernier recours, procéder à quelques vérifications ou faire un bilan des mots retenus au cours des lectures.

THE AUTHOR

Roald Dahl was born in Wales in 1916 of Norwegian parents and educated at an English public school. When he was eighteen, he started working for the Shell Oil Company in London. After four years, the company sent him to Africa.

When the Second World War broke out he enlisted in the Royal Air Force. He served as a fighter-pilot in Libya, Syria, Greece, Egypt and Iraq. After being seriously wounded when his plane was shot down in the Libyan desert, he was transferred to Washington where he became an Assistant Air Attaché. It was there that he started writing short stories based on his wartime experiences. They were first published in American magazines, and later as a book, *Over To You*.

Since then he has written many books of short stories, among which are *Someone Like You, Kiss Kiss, Twenty-Nine Kisses from Roald Dahl* and *Switch Bitch*. Some of his stories have been dramatized for television in a series called *Bizarre, Bizarre* and published in Penguin books as *Tales of the Unexpected* and *More Tales of the Unexpected*. His other publications include his novel *My Uncle Oswald, The Best of Roald Dahl* (a collection of his finest short stories), *Boy* and *Going Solo* (a sort of autobiography in two volumes) and *Two Fables*. He has also written a lot of children's books with strange and marvellous characters. A few titles are *James and the Giant Peach, Charlie and the Chocolate Factory, George's Marvellous Medicine, Danny the Champion of the World, The Twits* and his latest, *Matilda* (published in 1989).

11

The atmosphere, in Roald Dahl's stories, is disconcerting. The characters are apparently ordinary human beings, but their strange behaviour gradually reveals a particular weakness or obsession. There is a lot of betting and gambling among the characters and suspense plays a major part in the plot, with often a reversal of the situation towards the end.

Roald Dahl is a master of suspense and black humour and the reader will feel amused, moved, disconcerted, shocked or even outraged... but fascinated by his short stories.

THE HITCH-HIKER

A hitch-hiker can be a nuisance or an interesting travelling companion. Michael Fish is both. That strange and fascinating character turns out to be an extremely helpful partner, after all!

I had a new car. It was an exciting toy, a big B.M.W. 3.3 Li, which means 3.3 litre, long wheelbase, fuel injection. It had a top speed of 129 m.p.h. and terrific acceleration. The body was pale blue. The seats inside were darker blue and they were made of leather, genuine soft leather of the finest quality. The windows were electrically operated and so was the sun-roof. The radio aerial popped up when I switched on the radio, and disappeared when I switched it off. The powerful engine growled and grunted impatiently at slow
10 speeds, but at sixty miles an hour the growling stopped and the motor began to purr with pleasure.

I was driving up to London by myself. It was a lovely June day. They were haymaking in the fields and there were buttercups along both sides of the road. I was whispering along at seventy miles an hour, leaning back comfortably in my seat, with no more than a couple of fingers resting lightly on the wheel to keep her steady. Ahead of me I saw a man thumbing a lift. I touched the footbrake and brought the car to a stop beside him. I always stopped for hitch-
20 hikers. I knew just how it used to feel to be standing on the side of a country road watching the cars go by. I hated the drivers for pretending they didn't see me, especially the ones in big cars with three empty seats. The large expensive cars seldom stopped. It was always the smaller ones that offered you a lift, or the old rusty ones, or the ones that were already crammed full of children and the driver would say, "I think we can squeeze in one more."

The hitch-hiker poked his head through the open window and said, "Going to London, guv'nor?"
30 "Yes," I said, "Jump in."

He got in and I drove on.

He was a small ratty-faced man with grey teeth. His eyes

14

new ≠ old □ **exciting**: fascinating □ **toy**: thing to play with
wheelbase: distance between the front and back axes
top: maximum □ **speed**: rapidity of movement □ **m.p.h.**: miles per
hour □ **body**: outside □ **seat(s)**: to sit; a seat □ **dark(er)** ≠ pale
made **of** □ **leather**: animal skin □ **genuine**: real □ **soft**: no hard,
smooth □ **the finest**: the best □ **operated**: worked □ **sun-roof**: *toit
ouvrant* □ **aerial**: antenna (Am.) □ **popped up**: appeared suddenly
□ **switched on**: turned on; on ≠ off
powerful: *puissant* □ **engine**: motor □ **growled and grunted**:
(sounds) an angry dog growls; a pig grunts □ **slow** ≠ fast
began: started □ **purr**: (sound) a cat purrs when pleased
driving: you drive a vehicle □ **by myself**: alone □ **lovely**: fine
haymaking: cutting and drying grass in the sun □ **field(s)**: *champ*
buttercup(s): *bouton d'or* □ **both**: the two □ **whispering**: speaking
quietly □ **leaning back**: sitting back (relaxed position)
with no more... steady: guiding the car ("her" personification) by
touching the **wheel** *(volant)* with only 2 or 3 fingers
thumbing a lift: raising his thumb, hitch-hiking □ **footbrake**: pedal
used to slow down □ **beside him**: next to him, by his side
I knew... feel: I remembered the impression I had in the past
country ≠ city □ **watching**: observing □ **go by**: pass by □ **hated**:
detested; hate sb. for doing sth.
empty: unoccupied, free □ **expensive**: costing a lot of money
seldom: rarely □ **smaller**: (comparative) ≠ larger, bigger
lift: free ride (cf. above) □ **rusty**: attacked by corrosion
crammed full: very full, overfull □ **children**: sing. child
squeeze in one more: force one more (another) person into the car
poked his head: pushed his head forward
guv'nor: (fam.) used for addressing a man of superior status
jump in: get (got, got) into the car quickly
drove on: drive, drove, driven ("on" expresses continuation)
ratty-faced: with a face like a rat's □ **teeth**: sing. tooth

15

were dark and quick and clever, like a rat's eyes, and his ears were slightly pointed at the top. He had a cloth cap on his head and he was wearing a greyish-coloured jacket with enormous pockets. The grey jacket, together with the quick eyes and the pointed ears, made him look more than anything like some sort of a huge human rat.

"What part of London are you headed for?" I asked him.

"I'm goin' right through London and out the other side," he said. "I'm goin' to Epsom, for the races. It's Derby Day today."

"So it is," I said. "I wish I were going with you. I love betting on horses."

"I never bet on horses," he said. "I don't even watch 'em run. That's a stupid silly business."

"Then why do you go?" I asked.

He didn't seem to like that question. His little ratty face went absolutely blank and he sat there staring straight ahead at the road, saying nothing.

"I expect you help to work the betting machines or something like that," I said.

"That's even sillier," he answered. "There's no fun working them lousy machines and selling tickets to mugs. Any fool could do that."

There was a long silence. I decided not to question him any more. I remembered how irritated I used to get in my hitch-hiking days when drivers kept asking *me* questions. Where are you going? Why are you going there? What's your job? Are you married? Do you have a girl-friend? What's her name? How old are you? And so on and so forth. I used to hate it.

"I'm sorry," I said. "It's none of my business what you

eye(s): organ of sight □ **quick, clever**: intelligent □ **ear(s)**: organ of hearing □ **slightly**: a little □ **cloth cap**: soft flat head-covering

greyish: slightly grey □ **jacket**: short coat

together with: combined with, in addition to

look (like): resemble □ **more than anything**: very much

huge: enormous, gigantic

headed for: or heading for: going to

right through: all the way across

Epsom: town in Surrey famous for its horse-**races** □ **Derby**: famous annual horse-race run at Epsom since 1780

so it is: that's right □ **I wish I were...**: expression of desire for sth. that can't be □ **betting**: risking money (on sth.)

even: for emphasis (with negative) □ **watch'em**: look at them

run: to run; a race □ **silly business**: stupid activity

then: so, in that case

seem (+ infinitive): appear (+ infinitive) □ **like**: appreciate

went blank: became expressionless □ **staring straight ahead**: looking fixedly in front of him □ **saying nothing**: silent, mute

I expect: I suppose □ **help**: give assistance □ **work**: operate

sillier: comparative of "silly" □ **fun**: amusement

lousy: (sl.) awful □ **selling**: giving in return for money □ **mug(s)**: (sl.) foolish person □ **any**: every, no matter which

not to question him: "not" before the infinitive in the negative

any more: any longer □ **used to**: (past habit) □ **get (irritated)**: become exasperated □ **days**: period □ **kept**: keep + ing, persist in + ing

job: occupation, work □ **married?** or single? □ **girl-friend**: usual female companion of a man □ **so on and so forth**: etc

it's none of my business: it doesn't concern me

do. The trouble is, I'm a writer, and most writers are terrible nosey parkers."

"You write books?" he asked.

"Yes."

"Writin' books is okay," he said. "It's what I call a skilled trade. I'm in a skilled trade too. The folks I despise is them that spend all their lives doin' crummy old routine jobs with no skill in em' at all. You see what I mean?"

"Yes."

10   "The secret of life," he said, "is to become very very good at somethin' that's very very 'ard to do."

"Like you," I said.

"Exactly. You and me both."

"What makes you think that *I'm* any good at my job?" I asked. "There's an awful lot of bad writers around."

"You wouldn't be drivin' about in a car like this if you weren't no good at it," he answered. "It must've cost a tidy packet, this little job."

"It wasn't cheap."

20   "What can she do flat out?" he asked.

"One hundred and twenty-nine miles an hour," I told him.

"I'll bet she won't do it."

"I'll bet she will."

"All car makers is liars," he said. "You can buy any car you like and it'll never do what the makers say it will in the ads."

"This one will."

"Open 'er up then and prove it," he said. "Go on, 30 guv'nor, open 'er right up and let's see what she'll do."

There is a roundabout at Chalfont St Peter and immediately beyond it there's a long straight section of dual

trouble: problem □ **most**: the majority of, nearly all
nosey (or nosy) parker(s): (fam.) inquisitive person, one who sticks his (her) nose into other people's business

call: consider □ **skilled trade**: job requiring special skill (= talent, aptitude) □ **folks**: (fam.) people □ **despise**: regard as inferior
spend one's life: (pl. **lives**) doing sth. □ **crummy**: (fam.) of little value □ **at all**: (for emphasis) □ **you see what I mean?**: do you understand me?; mean, meant, meant; the meaning of sth.
good **at** sth. (note the preposition)
'ard: hard, difficult; ≠ easy
said: say, said, said; say sth. to sb., tell sb. sth.
exactly: quite right, as you say □ **you and me both**: the two of us
makes you think: leads you to think □ **any good**: good at all
an awful lot: (fam.) a great number □ **around**: in the profession
wouldn't (conditional) **if...** □ **about**: here and there
no good: (fam. and incorrect) any good □ **it must've cost**: you must have paid (for it) □ **a tidy packet**: (fam.) a lot □ **job**: thing
it wasn't cheap: (understatement) it was quite expensive
flat out: (fam.) at full speed
one hundred **and** twenty nine □ **told**: tell, told, told (sth., a story)

I'll bet: I'm sure (the hitch-hiker is challenging the driver)
I'll bet...: (the driver takes up the challenge)
car maker(s): car manufacturer □ **is** instead of are □ **liar(s)**: one who tells lies (= untrue things) □ **you like**: you want
ad(s) or advert: (short for advertisement) publicity for a product

open'er up: (fam.) accelerate □ **go on**: excl. of encouragement
right: completely □ **let's see**: imperative (1st person pl.)
roundabout: road junction where traffic goes round a central island
beyond: after □ **straight**: direct, not sinuous

19

carriageway. We came out of the roundabout on to the carriageway and I pressed my foot down on the accelerator. The big car leaped forward as though she'd been stung. In ten seconds or so, we were doing ninety.

"Lovely!" he cried. "Beautiful! Keep goin'!"

I had the accelerator jammed right down against the floor and I held it there.

"One hundred!" he shouted... "A hundred and five! ... A hundred and ten! ... A hundred and fifteen! Go on! Don't
10 slack off!"

I was in the outside lane and we flashed past several cars as though they were standing still — a green Mini, a big cream-coloured Citroën, a white Land-Rover, a huge truck with a container on the back, an orange-coloured Volkswagen Minibus...

"A hundred and twenty!" my passenger shouted, jumping up and down. "Go on! Go on! Get 'er up to one-two-nine!"

At that moment, I heard the scream of a police siren. It
20 was so loud it seemed to be right inside the car, and then a policeman on a motor-cycle loomed up alongside us on the inside lane and went past us and raised a hand for us to stop.

"Oh, my sainted aunt!" I said. "That's torn it!"

The policeman must have been doing about a hundred and thirty when he passed us, and he took plenty of time slowing down. Finally, he pulled into the side of the road and I pulled in behind him. "I didn't know police motor-cycles could go as fast as that," I said rather lamely.
30   "That one can," my passenger said. "It's the same make as yours. It's a B.M.W. R90S. Fastest bike on the road. That's what they're usin' nowadays."

dual carriageway : road with two lanes on each side and a division in the middle □ **pressed** : pushed, applied pressure
leaped forward : jumped ahead □ **as though** : as if □ **stung** : bitten ; sting, stung, stung (insect) □ **or so** : approximately
cried : exclaimed, shouted □ **keep goin'!** : go on ! don't stop !
jammed... floor : pressed at the maximum so that it was touching the floor □ **held** : kept ; hold, held, held

slack off or slacken off : reduce speed
outside lane : lane for fast traffic □ **flashed past** : passed as quickly as a flash □ **still** : immobile □ **Mini** : type of British car
cream-coloured : yellowish white □ **truck** : lorry
container : large box for transporting goods at the **back** (≠ the front) of a vehicle

jumping up and down : moving upwards and downwards alternately (sign of excitement) □ **one-two-nine** : 129 miles an hour
heard : hear, heard, heard □ **scream** : loud piercing sound
loud : great in volume □ **seemed** : appeared □ **inside** ≠ outside
loomed up : appeared suddenly □ **alongside us** : by our side
went past us : overtook us □ **raised a hand... to stop** : put his hand up in the air, signalling us to stop
"my sainted aunt !" (fam.) : excl. of surprise □ **"that's torn it !"** : (fam.) that ruins everything □ **must have...** : (supposition)
took : take, took, taken (one's time) □ **plenty of** : a lot of, lots of
slowing down : reducing speed □ **pulled into... road** : moved to the side of the road and stopped
as fast as that : (comparative) so fast □ **rather** : quite □ **lamely** : unconvincingly □ **same (as)** : ≠ different from □ **make** : trademark
fastest : (superlative) quickest □ **bike** : (fam.) short for motorbike
usin' : employing □ **nowadays** ≠ in the past

The policeman got off his motor-cycle and leaned the machine sideways on to its prop stand. Then he took off his gloves and placed them carefully on the seat. He was in no hurry now. He had us where he wanted us and he knew it.

"This is real trouble," I said. "I don't like it one bit."

"Don't talk to 'im any more than is necessary, you understand," my companion said. "Just sit tight and keep mum."

Like an executioner approaching his victim, the police-
10 man came strolling slowly towards us. He was a big meaty man with a belly, and his blue breeches were skintight around his enormous thighs. His goggles were pulled up on the helmet, showing a smouldering red face with wide cheeks.

We sat there like guilty schoolboys, waiting for him to arrive.

"Watch out for this man," my passenger whispered. "Ee looks mean as the devil."

The policeman came round to my open window and
20 placed one meaty hand on the sill. "What's the hurry?" he said.

"No hurry, officer," I answered.

"Perhaps there's a woman in the back having a baby and you're rushing her to hospital? Is that it?"

"No, officer."

"Or perhaps your house is on fire and you're dashing home to rescue the family from upstairs?" His voice was dangerously soft and mocking.

"My house isn't on fire, officer."

30 "In that case," he said, "you've got yourself into a nasty mess, haven't you? Do you know what the speed limit is in this country?"

22

got off: get off ≠ get on (a vehicle) □ **leaned... sideways**: put the bike in an oblique position □ **prop stand**: support

glove(s): protection for the hand □ **carefully**: with attention

hurry: haste □ **... wanted us**: we were at his mercy

real trouble: (fam.) a very bad situation □ **one bit**: (fam.) at all

talk: speak

sit tight: don't move □ **keep mum**: keep quiet, don't speak

executioner: one who executes a condemned person

strolling: walking in a relaxed manner □ **meaty**: fat, heavy

belly: *bedaine* □ **breeches**: trousers □ **skintight**: close-fitting

thigh(s): top part of the leg □ **goggles**: protection for the eyes

helmet: protection for the head □ **smouldering**: containing his fury

□ **wide**: big □ **cheek(s)**: part of the face below the eye

guilty: who have commited an offence □ **waiting...**: note the structure: to wait for sb. to do sth.

watch out: be careful, be on your guard; watch out for...

mean: cruel, unkind, nasty □ **devil**: evil spirit, Satan

sill: horizontal piece at the base of the window

officer: term used when addressing a policeman

perhaps: maybe (supposition) □ **having a baby**: giving birth

rushing her: taking her very quickly

on fire: burning □ **dashing**: hurrying, rushing

rescue: save □ **upstairs**: the upper floor in a house

soft: gentle, moderate □ **mocking**: ironical; mock sb. or at sb.

... nasty mess: (fam.) you've put yourself into a very difficult situation □ **speed limit**: fastest speed permitted by law □ **in this country**: in England; country, pl. countries

"Seventy," I said.

"And do you mind telling me exactly what speed you were doing just now?"

I shrugged and didn't say anything.

When he spoke next, he raised his voice so loud that I jumped. *"One hundred and twenty miles per hour!"* he barked. "That's *fifty* miles an hour over the limit!"

He turned his head and spat out a big gob of spit. It landed on the wing of my car and started sliding down over
10 my beautiful blue paint. Then he turned back again and stared hard at my passenger. "And who are you?" he asked sharply.

"He's a hitch-hiker," I said. "I'm giving him a lift."

"I didn't ask you," he said. "I asked him."

"'Ave I done somethin' wrong?" my passenger asked. His voice was as soft and oily as haircream.

"That's more than likely," the policeman answered. "Anyway, you're a witness. I'll deal with you in a minute. Driving-licence," he snapped, holding out his hand.
20 I gave him my driving-licence.

He unbuttoned the left-hand breast-pocket of his tunic and brought out the dreaded books of tickets. Carefully, he copied the name and address from my licence. Then he gave it back to me. He strolled round to the front of the car and read the number from the number-plate and wrote that down as well. He filled in the date, the time and the details of my offence. Then he tore out the top copy of the ticket. But before handing it to me, he checked that all the information had come through clearly on his own carbon
30 copy. Finally, he replaced the book in his tunic pocket and fastened the button.

"Now you," he said to my passenger, and he walked

seventy m.p.h : approximately 110 km an hour (112,6)
do you mind + ing : (polite request) would you like + infinitive

shrugged : raised my shoulders *(épaules)* as a sign of ignorance
next : just after □ **raised... so loud** : adopted such a loud tone of voice ; raise one's voice, speak up
barked : said sharply ; dogs bark □ **over** : above, beyond
spat : ejected from his mouth ; to spit □ **gob of spit** : (fam.) lump of saliva □ **landed** : fell □ **wing** : *aile* □ **sliding down** : running down
paint : colouring substance
stared hard : looked fixedly and intensely
sharply : abruptly

somethin' instead of anything (fam. language) □ **wrong** : bad
as (adj.) **as** : (comparison) □ **oily** : unctuous □ **haircream** : hair gel
likely : probable
witness : sb. who has seen sth. happen □ **deal with you** : consider your case □ **licence** : permit □ **snapped** : said sharply
gave : give, gave, given ; give sb. sth. or give sth. to sb.
unbuttoned : undid □ **left-hand breast-pocket** : pocket situated at the top on the left □ **dread(ed)** : fear, anxiety □ **ticket(s)** : (fam.) official notification of a driving or parking offence
back : give sth. back to sb., return sth. to sb.
number-plate : plate showing the registration number of the car
write (**wrote, written**) sth. **down** □ **as well** : too □ **filled in** : wrote
tore out : removed, ripped out □ **top copy** : 1st copy, original
handing : giving ("before" + ing) □ **checked** : verified
information : (no s !) □ **had come through** : was visible □ **own** : (possession) □ **finally** : in the end □ **replaced** : put back
fastened the button ≠ unbuttoned (1. 21)
now you : it's your turn now, I'm going to deal with you now

25

around to the other side of the car. From the other breast-pocket he produced a small black notebook. "Name?" he snapped.

"Michael Fish," my passenger said.

"Address?"

"Fourteen, Windsor Lane, Luton."

"Show me something to prove this is your real name and address," the policeman said.

My passenger fished in his pockets and came out with a 10 driving-licence of his own. The policeman checked the name and address and handed it back to him.

"What's your job?" he asked sharply.

"I'm an 'od carrier."

"A *what?*"

"An 'od carrier."

"Spell it."

"H-O-D C-A-..."

"That'll do. And what's a hod carrier, may I ask?"

"An 'od carrier, officer, is a person 'oo carries the cement 20 up the ladder to the bricklayer. And the 'od is what 'ee carries it in. It's got a long 'andle, and on the top you've got two bits of wood set at an angle..."

"All right, all right. Who's your employer?"

"Don't 'ave one. I'm unemployed."

The policeman wrote all this down in the black note-book. Then he returned the book to its pocket and did up the button.

"When I get back to the station I'm going to do a little checking up on you," he said to my passenger.

30 "Me? What've I done wrong?" the rat-faced man asked.

"I don't like your face, that's all," the policeman said.

26

produced: brought out □ **notebook**: small book in which notes can be written

Michael: (first name, Christian name, forename) □ **Fish** (surname)

address: (double d!) what's your address? where do you live?

Lane: (capital "l") alley □ **Luton**: town in Bedfordshire

show me: let me see □ **sth. to prove**: a proof □ **real**: true ≠ false

fished: (fam.) searched; to fish keys out of a pocket

of his own: that was his, that belonged to him

'od carrier: (read on for the explanation of this word)

a what?: (he doesn't understand the word, he needs an explanation) "pardon?" is more formal

spell (spelt, spelt or spelled): name the letters of the word one after the other; a spelling mistake (in a dictation...)

that'll do: that's enough □ **may I ask?**: polite expression (ironical, here) □ **'oo**: who □ **carries**: passes □ **cement**: *ciment*

ladder: *échelle* □ **a bricklayer** builds walls, etc. with bricks □ **what... it in**: the thing he uses to carry it □ **'andle**: handle (to hold it) □ **bit(s)**: piece □ **wood**: (from trees) □ **set**: fixed

all right: (he is getting impatient) □ **employer**: boss (fam.); employees work for employers □ **unemployed**: out of work, jobless

all this: all this information, every detail

its: possessive adjective □ **did up**: fastened; do, did, done

get back: return (no future after "when") □ **police station**

I'm going to...: he expresses his intention □ **checking up**: verification, investigation, inquiry □ **wrong**: bad, illegal; do sth. wrong, commit an offence

that's all: and nothing else, and nothing more

"And we just might have a picture of it somewhere in our files." He strolled round the car and returned to my window.

"I suppose you know you're in serious trouble," he said to me.

"Yes, officer."

"You won't be driving this fancy car of yours again for a very long time, not after *we've* finished with you. You won't be driving *any* car again come to that for several
10 years. And a good thing, too. I hope they lock you up for a spell into the bargain."

"You mean prison?" I asked, alarmed.

"Absolutely," he said, smacking his lips. "In the clink. Behind the bars. Along with all the other criminals who break the law. *And* a hefty fine into the bargain. Nobody will be more pleased about that than me. I'll see you in court, both of you. You'll be getting a summons to appear."

He turned away and walked over to his motor-cycle. He flipped the prop stand back into position with his foot and
20 swung his leg over the saddle. Then he kicked the starter and roared off up the road out of sight.

"Phew!" I gasped. "That's done it."

"We was caught," my passenger said. "We was caught good and proper."

"I was caught, you mean."

"That's right," he said. "What you goin' to do now, guv'nor?"

"I'm going straight up to London to talk to my solicitor," I said. I started the car and drove on.
30 "You mustn't believe what 'ee said to you about goin' to prison," my passenger said. "They don't put nobody in the clink just for speedin'."

might: expresses possibility □ **picture**: photo(graph)
file(s): collection of documents

you know: you realize □ **in serious trouble**: in a critical situation; be in trouble, get into trouble

won't: future (neg.) □ **fancy**: special, de luxe □ **(car) of yours**: your car □ **time**: period □ **after** ≠ before
any car at all □ **come to that**: in fact □ **several**: some
year(s): 12 months □ **I hope**: I wish □ **lock** (sb.) **up**: imprison
a spell: some time □ **into the bargain**: in addition to everything else
alarmed: apprehensive, worried
smacking his lips: *se léchant les babines* □ **clink**: (sl.) prison
behind ≠ in front of □ **along with**: together with
break: don't respect □ **hefty**: big □ **fine**: sum paid as a penalty
more... than: (comparative) □ **pleased**: happy □ **court**: tribunal
getting: receiving □ **summons**: order to appear in court
away: in the opposite direction □ **over to**: towards
flipped... foot (pl. feet): *ôta la béquille (à l'aide de son pied)*
swung... saddle: moved his leg up and over the seat □ **kicked** with his foot □ **roared off**: drove off noisily □ **out of sight** ≠ in view
gasped: puffed, panted □ **that's done it**: everything is ruined
we was: fam. for "we were" □ **caught**: catch, caught, caught
good and proper: (fam.) completely

right: correct, true □ **what you...**: fam. for "what are you..."

straight: immediately □ **talk to**: discuss with □ **solicitor**: lawyer who gives advice on legal matters
believe sth.: take sth. seriously
nobody: instead of anybody, anyone (familiar language)
speedin': speeding: going faster than the legal limit

29

"Are you sure of that?" I asked.

"I'm positive," he answered. "They can take your licence away and they can give you a whoppin' big fine, but that'll be the end of it."

I felt tremendously relieved.

"By the way," I said, "why did you lie to him?"

"Who, me?" he said. "What makes you think I lied?"

"You told him you were an unemployed hod carrier. But you told *me* you were in a highly-skilled trade."

10 "So I am," he said. "But it don't pay to tell everythin' to a copper."

"So what *do* you do?" I asked him.

"Ah," he said slyly. "That'd be tellin', wouldn't it?"

"Is it something you're ashamed of?"

"Ashamed?" he cried. "Me, ashamed of my job? I'm about as proud of it as anybody could be in the entire world!"

"Then why won't you tell me?"

"You writers really is nosey parkers, aren't you?" he said.
20 "And you ain't goin' to be 'appy, I don't think, until you've found out exactly what the answer is?"

"I don't really care one way or the other," I told him, lying.

He gave me a crafty little ratty look out of the sides of his eyes. "I think you do care," he said. "I can see it in your face that you think I'm in some kind of a very peculiar trade and you're just achin' to know what it is."

I didn't like the way he read my thoughts. I kept quiet and stared at the road ahead.

30 "You'd be right, too," he went on. "I *am* in a very peculiar trade. I'm in the queerest peculiar trade of 'em all."

30

sure: certain; be sure of sth.; be sure that...
positive: sure □ **they**: (indefinite) the judges or the police □ **take (sth.) away**: confiscate, seize □ **whoppin' big**: (fam.) very big □ **that'll be the end of it**: that's all they can do
feel, **felt**, felt □ **tremendously**: extremely □ **relieved**: free from anxiety □ **by the way**: *au fait* □ **lie**: tell a lie ≠ tell the truth
lied: (note: lie, lied and lie, lay, lain, are two different verbs)

highly: (intensifier) very
so I am: that's true □ **it don't pay**: (fam.) it doesn't pay, there is no advantage in + ing □ **copper**: (sl.) policeman, bobby (fam.)
so: then, in that case
slyly: playfully, mischievously □ **that'd be tellin'**: you would like to know □ be **ashamed** (of sth.): suffer from a feeling of shame or inferiority □ **cried**: shouted
proud of ≠ ashamed of; a feeling of pride or superiority □ **in the entire world**: in the whole world, on earth (our planet)
why won't you + verb: why don't you want to + verb ("won't" is used to express refusal) □ **is** instead of are (familiar)
ain't: aren't (also: am not, isn't, hasn't, haven't) □ **until**: before
found out: discovered □ **the answer** to the question
I don't care: it doesn't matter to me □ **one way or the other**: if I know the answer or if I don't □ **lying**: cf. lie (1. 6-7)
crafty: artful, cunning (as a fox), shrewd □ **side(s)**: corner
you do care: it's important to you ("do" for emphasis)
some kind (sort) **of a...** (very imprecise) □ **peculiar**: unusual, strange
achin': (fam.) impatient, anxious, dying (fam.)
way: manner □ **read my thoughts**: could read my mind
you'd be: you would be (meaning: you are) □ **went on**: continued
the queerest: (superlative) the strangest, the most peculiar □ **of'em** (them) **all**: all of trades

I waited for him to go on.

"That's why I 'as to be extra careful 'oo I'm talkin' to, you see. 'Ow am I to know, for instance, you're not another copper in plain clothes?"

"Do I look like a copper?"

"No," he said. "You don't. And you ain't. Any fool could tell that."

He took from his pocket a tin of tobacco and a packet of cigarette papers and started to roll a cigarette. I was
10 watching him out of the corner of one eye, and the speed with which he performed this rather difficult operation was incredible. The cigarette was rolled and ready in about five seconds. He ran his tongue along the edge of the paper, stuck it down and popped the cigarette between his lips. Then, as if from nowhere, a lighter appeared in his hand. The lighter flamed. The cigarette was lit. The lighter disappeared. It was altogether a remarkable performance.

"I've never seen anyone roll a cigarette as fast as that,"
20 I said.

"Ah," he said, taking a deep suck of smoke. "So you noticed."

"Of course I noticed. It was quite fantastic."

He sat back and smiled. It pleased him very much that I had noticed how quickly he could roll a cigarette. "You want to know what makes me able to do it?" he asked.

"Go on then."

"It's because I've got fantastic fingers. These fingers of mine," he said, holding up both hands high in front of him,
30 "are quicker and cleverer than the fingers of the best piano player in the world!"

"Are you a piano player?"

32

waited: note the construction: to wait for sb. to do sth.
I'as (= have) **to be**: (obligation) □ **extra** + adj.: exceptionally
'ow am I to know: how can I know □ **for instance**: for example
in plain clothes ≠ in uniform

any fool could tell that: it is so evident that anybody would notice
it (even a fool! = a stupid person)
take, **took**, taken □ **tin**: metal box □ you buy **tobacco** for pipes and
cigarettes at the tobacconist's □ **started**: began

performed: accomplished (a performance) □ **rather**: quite
incredible: unbelievable □ **ready** for smoking
ran: moved □ **tongue**: long muscle in the mouth □ **edge**: border
stuck: cf. stick, fix □ **popped**: put quickly □ **lip(s)**: upper lip ; lower
lip □ **a lighter** gives light (not fire!) □ **appeared**: was seen ; ≠
disappeared □ **lit**: light, lit, lit or lighted
altogether: absolutely □ **remarkable**: extraordinary, exceptional,
unusual □ **performance**: execution, achievement
never: not once before now

taking a deep suck of smoke: inhaling the cigarette-smoke deeply
(with insistance) □ **noticed**: noted, remarked
of course: certainly □ **quite**: absolutely
smiled: looked happy □ **pleased**: satisfied □ **very much**: a lot
could: was able to (capacity, ability)
makes me able to + verb: enables me to..., gives me the capacity
to... □ **go on**: tell me (encouragement to speak)
finger(s): we have ten fingers (five on each hand)
holding up: keeping up, raising □ **high** (up): ≠ low (down)
quicker and cleverer (comparatives) □ **the best**: superlative of
"good" □ **in** (not of!) □ **the world**: that exists
pianoplayer: pianist ; guitar player, guitarist...

"Don't be daft," he said. "Do I look like a piano player?"

I glanced at his fingers. They were so beautifully shaped, so slim and long and elegant, they didn't seem to belong to the rest of him at all. They looked more like the fingers of a brain surgeon or a watchmaker.

"My job," he went on, "is a hundred times more difficult than playin' the piano. Any twerp can learn to do that. There's titchy little kids learnin' to play the piano in almost
10 any 'ouse you go into these days. That's right, ain't it?"

"More or less," I said.

"Of course it's right. But there's not one person in ten million can learn to do what I do. Not one in ten million! 'Ow about that?"

"Amazing," I said.

"You're darn right it's amazin'," he said.

"I think I know what you do," I said. "You do conjuring tricks. You're a conjurer."

"Me?" he snorted. "A conjurer? Can you picture me
20 goin' round crummy kids' parties makin' rabbits come out of top 'ats?"

"Then you're a card player. You get people into card games and deal yourself marvellous hands."

"Me! A rotten card-sharper!" he cried. "That's a miserable racket if ever there was one."

"All right. I give up."

I was taking the car along slowly now, at no more than forty miles an hour, to make quite sure I wasn't stopped again. We had come on to the main London-Oxford road
30 and were running down the hill towards Denham.

Suddenly, my passenger was holding up a black leather belt in his hand. "Ever seen this before?" he asked. The belt

daft: stupid, silly

glanced (at): gave a quick look (at) □ **shaped:** formed
slim: thin ≠ fat □ **belong to:** be part of
the rest of him: the rest of his body
a brain surgeon or a watchmaker: a doctor who operates on the
brain (head) or sb. who makes watches and clocks □ **100 times:**
a lot □ (play) **the** + instrument □ **twerp:** (sl.) idiot □ **learn** ≠ teach
titchy: (sl.) very small □ **kid(s):** (fam.) child □ **almost:** nearly
these days: nowadays □ **that's right:** it's true
more or less: approximately
in ten million (no s!): out of ten million (percentage)
can learn: who can learn ("who" is omitted)
'ow (= how) **about that?:** what about that? What do you think of
it? □ **amazing:** very surprising, astonishing, stupefying
darn: or darned: euphemistic word for "damn" or "damned" (sl.),
absolutely
a conjurer (or conjuror) does **conjuring tricks** (= magic)
snorted: said angrily, grumbled □ **picture:** imagine
parties: birthday party, etc. □ **rabbit(s):** animal with long ears!
top'at(s): top hat (tall elegant black hat)
a card player plays card games (poker...) □ **get people into:**
influence people to play □ **deal** cards: distribute □ **hand(s):** set of
cards □ **rotten:** disloyal □ a **card-sharper** plays cards dishonestly
miserable: infamous □ **racket:** dishonest enterprise
I give up: I stop trying to find (or guess) the answer

to make quite sure: to (in order to) be absolutely certain
again: once more □ **main:** principal, most important
hill: elevation of the land □ **towards:** in the direction of
holding up: brandishing □ **leather:** cf. page 15, 1. 5
belt: thing to hold trousers up □ (have you) **ever seen...?**

35

had a brass buckle of unusual design.

"Hey!" I said. "That's mine, isn't it? It *is* mine! Where did you get it?"

He grinned and waved the belt gently from side to side. "Where d'you think I got it?" he said. "Off the top of your trousers, of course."

I reached down and felt for my belt. It was gone.

"You mean you took it off me while we've been driving along?" I asked, flabbergasted.

10   He nodded, watching me all the time with those little black ratty eyes.

"That's impossible," I said. "You'd have to undo the buckle and slide the whole thing out through the loops all the way round. I'd have seen you doing it. And even if I hadn't seen you, I'd have felt it."

"Ah, but you didn't, did you?" he said, triumphant. He dropped the belt on his lap, and now all at once there was a brown shoelace dangling from his fingers. "And what about this, then?" he exclaimed, waving the shoelace.

20   "What about it?" I said.

"Anyone round 'ere missin' a shoelace?" he asked, grinning.

I glanced down at my shoes. The lace of one of them was missing. "Good grief!" I said. "How did you do that? I never saw you bending down."

"You never saw nothin'," he said proudly. "You never even saw me move an inch. And you know why?"

"Yes," I said. "Because you've got fantastic fingers."

"Exactly right!" he cried. "You catch on pretty quick,
30 don't you?" He sat back and sucked away at his homemade cigarette, blowing the smoke out in a thin stream against the windshield. He knew he had impressed me greatly with

36

brass buckle: *boucle en laiton* □ **unusual design**: uncommon decorative pattern □ **mine**: (possessive pronoun) my belt

get: find, obtain; get, got, got

grinned: smiled (wide smile) □ **waved**: moved □ **from side to side**: from left to right, to and fro □ **off**: from (idea of removal); take (took, taken) off, take away, remove

reached down: moved my hand down □ **felt for**: tried to touch □ **it was gone**: it had disappeared □ **while**: during the time that

flabbergasted: (fam.) stupefied, amazed, astounded

nodded: made a sign of agreement (meaning "yes") with his head

you'd have to: you would need to (necessity) □ **undo**: open

slide, slid, slid: pass □ **whole**: entire □ **thing**: belt □ **loop(s)**: *passant* □ **all the way**: completely □ **even if**: supposing

felt: feel (felt, felt), experience a sensation

triumphant: victorious, exultant

dropped: let fall □ **on his lap**: *sur ses genoux* □ **all at once**: immediately □ **shoelace**: cord (lace) on a shoe □ **dangling**: hanging freely; keys dangling from a chain □ **waving**: cf. 1. 4

anyone... shoelace: is there anybody in this place who has lost (lose, lost, lost) a shoelace? (ironical)

missing: not there □ **good grief!**: exclamation of surprise

never: (emphatic) □ **bending down**: moving downwards

nothin': for "anything" □ **proudly**: with pride (self-esteem)

inch: (measure of length) 2,54 cm ; a foot = 12 inches

catch on: understand □ **pretty quick**: (fam.) quite rapidly

sucked away at: drew (the smoke) into his mouth □ **homemade**: self-made □ **blowing out** ≠ inhaling □ **stream** of smoke, water...

windshield (Am.): windscreen, *pare-brise* □ **greatly**: very much

those two tricks, and this made him very happy. "I don't want to be late," he said. "What time is it?"

"There's a clock in front of you," I told him.

"I don't trust car clocks," he said. "What does your watch say?"

I hitched up my sleeve to look at the watch on my wrist. It wasn't there. I looked at the man. He looked back at me, grinning.

"You've taken that, too," I said.

10 He held out his hand and there was my watch lying in his palm. "Nice bit of stuff, this," he said. "Superior quality. Eighteen-carat gold. Easy to flog, too. It's never any trouble gettin' rid of quality goods."

"I'd like it back, if you don't mind," I said rather huffily.

He placed the watch carefully on the leather tray in front of him. "I wouldn't nick anything from you, guv'nor," he said. "You're my pal. You're giving me a lift."

"I'm glad to hear it," I said.

20 "All I'm doin' is answerin' your questions," he went on. "You asked me what I did for a livin' and I'm showin' you."

"What else have you got of mine?"

He smiled again, and now he started to take from the pocket of his jacket one thing after another that belonged to me — my driving-licence, a key-ring with four keys on it, some pound notes, a few coins, a letter from my publishers, my diary, a stubby old pencil, a cigarette-lighter, and last of all, a beautiful old sapphire ring with pearls

30 around it belonging to my wife. I was taking the ring up to the jeweller in London because one of the pearls was missing.

tricks: cf. page 35, 1. 18

be late ≠ be on time or in time

clock: instrument for measuring and showing time

I don't trust: I have no confidence in □ **what does your watch say?** what time is it by your watch? (= small clock usually worn on the **wrist**) □ **hitched up**: pulled up □ **sleeve**: part of the shirt that covers the arm

too: also, in addition, as well

held out: extended; hold, held, held

palm: inside of the hand □ **nice bit of stuff**: (sl.) lovely article

gold: precious yellow metal □ **flog**: (sl.): sell

gettin' rid of: (here) selling □ **goods**: (plural) articles

I'd like (to have) **it back** □ **if you don't mind**: if you please (sarcastic) □ **rather**: somewhat □ **huffily**: angrily

placed: put □ **tray**: flat surface to put things on

nick sth. from sb.: (sl.) take dishonestly, steal (stole, stolen)

pal: (fam.) friend; he's an old pal of mine

glad: happy, pleased, delighted; ≠ unhappy, sad

all: the only thing □ **went on**: continued (to speak)

for a livin': what do you do for a living? what's your job?

what else: what other thing; what else would you like?

that belonged to me: that was mine, that I owned = possessed

key-ring: thing on which keys (to open doors) are kept

pound note(s): bank note (value: 1 pound) □ **coin(s)**: metal disc (money) □ **publishers** issue books □ **diary**: *agenda* □ **stubby**: short and thick □ **last** ≠ first □ **ring**: ornament for the finger

wife: man's partner in marriage

the jeweller sells and repairs jewellery (rings, bracelets, necklaces, chains, medals, etc.)

"Now *there's* another lovely piece of goods," he said, turning the ring over in his fingers. "That's eighteenth century, if I'm not mistaken, from the reign of King George the Third."

"You're right," I said, impressed. "You're absolutely right."

He put the ring on the leather tray with the other items.

"So you're a pickpocket," I said.

"I don't like that word," he answered. "It's a coarse and vulgar word. Pickpockets is coarse and vulgar people who only do easy little amateur jobs. They lift money from blind old ladies."

"What do you call yourself, then?"

"Me? I'm a fingersmith. I'm a professional fingersmith." He spoke the words solemnly and proudly, as though he were telling me he was the President of the Royal College of Surgeons or the Archbishop of Canterbury.

"I've never heard that word before," I said. "Did you invent it?"

"Of course I didn't invent it," he replied. "It's the name given to them who's risen to the very top of the profession. You've 'eard of a goldsmith and a silversmith, for instance. They're experts with gold and silver. I'm an expert with my fingers, so I'm a fingersmith."

"It must be an interesting job."

"It's a marvellous job," he answered. "It's lovely."

"And that's why you go to the races?"

"Race meetings is easy meat," he said. "You just stand around after the race, watchin' for the lucky ones to queue up and draw their money. And when you see someone collectin' a big bundle of notes, you simply follows after 'im and 'elps yourself. But don't get me wrong, guv'nor. I never

40

piece (of goods): article, item; piece, portion (of cake, etc.)

eighteenth century: 1700 to 1800; a century = 100 years

mistaken: wrong; mistake, error □ **King** (not the!) **George the Third** (not three!) reigned from 1760 to 1820

right ≠ wrong; be right; that's right

items: thing (usually included in a list or collection)

a pickpocket steals things from people's pockets or bags

coarse: unrefined, indelicate, crude, rough

is: for "are"

lift: (fam.) steal □ **blind:** who can't see

old ladies: polite for "old women"

call: name; what are you called? what's your name?

fingersmith: (read on for the explanation of this word)

spoke: said; speak, spoke, spoken □ **solemnly:** with dignity

Surgeons perform medical operations □ **the Archbishop of Canterbury** (l'Archevêque de Cantorbéry) is the highest authority in the Church of England

replied: answered

them who's risen: those who have raised (= elevated) themselves; rise, rose, risen □ ('eard) **of:** hear of or about sth. □ **for instance:** for example □ **gold and silver** are precious metals (gold is yellow, silver is grey)

it must be: (supposition); she looks pale, she must be ill!

meeting(s): gathering of people □ **easy meat:** (fam.) simple

the lucky ones: people who have won some money □ **queue up:** stand in a queue (= line of people) □ **draw:** collect

bundle: pile □ **follows after'im:** follow him, go after him

'elps yourself: take money □ **get me wrong:** misunderstand me

41

takes nothin' from a loser. Nor from poor people neither. I only go after them as can afford it, the winners and the rich."

"That's very thoughtful of you," I said. "How often do you get caught?"

"Caught?" he cried, disgusted. "*Me* get caught! It's only pickpockets get caught. Fingersmiths never. Listen, I could take the false teeth out of your mouth if I wanted to and you wouldn't even catch me!"

10 "I don't have false teeth," I said.

"I know you don't," he answered. "Otherwise I'd 'ave 'ad 'em out long ago!"

I believed him. Those long slim fingers of his seemed able to do anything.

We drove on for a while without talking.

"That policeman's going to check up on you pretty thoroughly," I said. "Doesn't that worry you a bit?"

"Nobody's checkin' up on me," he said.

"Of course they are. He's got your name and address
20 written down most carefully in his black book."

The man gave me another of his sly, ratty little smiles. "Ah," he said. "So 'ee 'as. But I'll bet 'ee ain't got it all written down in 'is memory as well. I've never known a copper yet with a decent memory. Some of 'em can't even remember their own names."

"What's memory got to do with it?" I asked. "It's written down in his book, isn't it?"

"Yes, guv'nor, it is. But the trouble is, 'ee's lost the book. 'Ee's lost both books, the one with my name in it *and* the
30 one with yours."

In the long delicate fingers of his right hand, the man was holding up in triumph the two books he had taken from the

42

a loser: sb. who has lost money (lose ≠ win) □ **nor:** *ni...*
them as can afford it: those who have enough money
rich: wealthy; ≠ poor
thoughtful: considerate, courteous (ironical) □ **how often:** how
many times □ **get caught:** by the police; cf. catch
disgusted: outraged

false teeth: artificial teeth, denture

otherwise: if things were different □ **I'd 'ave 'ad 'em out:** I would
have taken them out □ **long ago:** a long time before now
believed: trusted; believe sth. or sb.; I don't believe you!
anything: everything
a while: a moment, some time □ **without talking:** in silence (note:
without + ing) □ **pretty + adj.:** (fam.) quite, rather
thoroughly: in detail □ **worry you a bit:** make you feel a little
uneasy (apprehensive)

most + adjective or adverb: very

so 'ee 'as: so he has, that's right
I've never known: I have not met (meet, met, met)
yet: up to now □ **decent:** good enough
remember: recall (through memory) □ **their own names:** ≠ other
people's names

trouble: problem □ **'ee's lost:** he has no longer got
the one: the book ("one" can replace any noun)
yours: (possessive pronoun) your name
right ≠ left

policeman's pockets. "Easiest job I ever done," he announced proudly.

I nearly swerved the car into a milk-truck, I was so excited.

"That copper's got nothin' on either of us now," he said.

"You're a genius!" I cried.

"Ee's got no names, no addresses, no car number, no nothin'," he said.

10 "You're brilliant!"

"I think you'd better pull in off this main road as soon as possible," he said. "Then we'd better build a little bonfire and burn these books."

"You're a fantastic fellow," I exclaimed.

"Thank you, guv'nor," he said. "It's always nice to be appreciated."

easiest: superlative of "easy" □ **I (have) ever done**: I have done up to this day

nearly: almost □ **swerved**: turned suddenly □ **milk-truck**: lorry transporting milk (from cows)

either of us: you and me

genius: (very strong word) Mozart and Einstein were geniuses

brilliant: (strong compliment) ingenious, very clever

you'd better: you should □ **pull in off**: leave □ **soon**: early

build (built, built): make □ **bonfire**: open-air fire

burn (burnt, burnt): destroy by means of a fire

fellow: (fam.) man, comrade

nice: pleasant, agreable

appreciated: recognized, esteemed (formal)

Grammaire au fil des nouvelles

Traduisez les phrases suivantes inspirées du texte (le premier chiffre renvoie aux pages, les suivants aux lignes) :

Les vitres étaient commandées électriquement et le toit ouvrant aussi (voix passive ; traduction de : aussi, non plus, 14 - 6,7).

C'était un petit homme au visage de rat et aux dents grises(adjectif composé ; *with* +caractéristique physique, 14 - 32).

Il avait une casquette de toile sur la tête (possessif devant une partie du corps, 16 - 2).

N'importe quel idiot pourrait le faire (conditionnel de *can* ; 16 - 24).

Je détestais cela autrefois (forme fréquentative : *used to*, 16 - 31).

Elle a dû coûter un sacré paquet, cette petite merveille (supposition : *must have* + p. passé, 18 - 17,18).

C'est la même marque que la vôtre (comparaison ; pronom possessif, 20 - 30,31).

Et vous pouvez me dire (= cela vous dérange-t-il de me dire) **exactement quelle vitesse vous faisiez à l'instant ?** (gérondif après certaines expressions ; p. *continuous*, 24 - 2,3).

Puis il me le rendit (ordre des compléments, 24 - 23,24).

Alors pourquoi ne voulez-vous pas me (le) dire ? (idée de refus : auxiliaire *won't*, 30 - 18).

Je pense *qu'en fait* ça vous préoccupe (formule emphatique, 30 - 25).

Je n'ai jamais vu personne rouler une cigarette aussi vite que cela (composés de *some, any, no* ; comparatif d'égalité, 32 - 19).

Et même si je ne vous avais pas vu, je l'aurais senti (conditionnel : *if…*, 36 - 14,15).

Le règne du roi George III (titres non précédés de l'article : chiffres numéraux ordinaux : *the first…* etc., 40 - 3,4).

Je n'ai encore jamais connu de flic qui ait (= avec) **une mémoire correcte** (*yet* + p. *perfect*, 42 - 23,24).

DEATH OF AN OLD MAN

Behind the toughness of the war-hero, the frailty of a
human being. _pensée_   _fragilité_

This story is from Roald Dahl's first book *Over To You*.
The ten stories included in the book are based on the
writer's experience as a wartime fighter-pilot, although the
introduction reads as follows:

"I do not refer to anyone in particular in these stories.
The names are not the names of pilots I have known; nor
does the use of the personal pronoun necessarily mean that
I am referring to myself."

Oh God, how I am frightened.

Now that I am alone I don't have to hide it; I don't have to hide anything any longer. I can let my face go because no one can see me; because there's twenty-one thousand feet between me and them and because now that it's happening again I couldn't pretend any more even if I wanted to. Now I don't have to press my teeth together and tighten the muscles of my jaw as I did during lunch when the corporal brought in the message; when he handed it to Tinker and

10 Tinker looked up at me and said, "Charlie, it's your turn. You're next up." As if I didn't know that. As if I didn't know that I was next up. As if I didn't know it last night when I went to bed, and at midnight when I was still awake and all the way through the night, at one in the morning and at two and three and four and five and six and at seven o'clock when I got up. As if I didn't know it while I was dressing and while I was having breakfast and while I was reading the magazines in the mess, playing shove-halfpenny in the mess, reading the notices in the mess, playing billiards in the

20 mess. I knew it then and I knew it when we went in to lunch, while we were eating that mutton for lunch. And when the corporal came into the room with the message —it wasn't anything at all. It wasn't anything more than when it begins to rain because there is a black cloud in the sky. When he handed the paper to Tinker I knew what Tinker was going to say before he had opened his mouth. I knew exactly what he was going to say.

So that wasn't anything either.

But when he folded the message up and put it in his

30 pocket and said, "Finish your pudding. You've got plenty of time," that was when it got worse, because I knew for certain then that it was going to happen again, that within

48

Oh God: (excl.) My God! □ **frightened:** afraid, terrified
alone: by myself □ **have to:** need to □ **hide:** conceal, keep secret
any longer: any more □ **let my face go:** be natural
there's a distance of □ **21.000 feet:** 6.400 m (1 foot = 30,48 cm)
between: separating □ **happening** (again): coming back
pretend: simulate □ **even:** (intensifier) □ **wanted to:** wished
press...: *serrer les dents* (1 tooth, 2 teeth) □ **tighten:** contract
jaw: bones in which the teeth are set (upper and lower jaw)
brought in: came in with (cf. bring) □ **handed:** gave
say, said, said □ **it's your turn:** time has come for you to go
next up: the following name on the list
last night: yesterday evening
midnight: 12 p.m. □ **still awake:** not asleep yet...
... through the night: all night long □ **one in the morning:** 1 a.m.

get up, got up, got up (from bed) □ **while:** when □ **dressing:** putting
my clothes on □ **breakfast:** first meal of the day
mess: (milit.) communal room □ **shove-halfpenny:** game played
with halfpenny coins *(palet de table)* □ **notice(s):** announcement
knew: was aware of; know, knew, known
lunch: light meal eaten in the middle of the day □ **mutton:** meat
from a sheep □ **came into:** entered (formal); come, came, come
at all (for emphasis) □ **begins:** starts
rain: the rain is the water that falls in drops from **clouds**
going to + verb (near future)
before ≠ after □ **mouth:** you open your mouth to speak

either: *non plus*
folded (up): you must fold a letter to put it in an envelope
pudding: dessert □ **plenty of:** a lot of, lots of □ **got** + adj.: became
worse: superlative of "bad"; ≠ better
then: at that moment □ **within:** before (a certain time)

half an hour I would be strapping myself in and testing the engine and signalling to the airmen to pull away the chocks. The others were all sitting around eating their pudding; mine was still on my plate in front of me, and I couldn't take another mouthful. But it was fine when I tightened my jaw muscles and said, "Thank God for that. I'm tired of sitting around here picking my nose." It was certainly fine when I said that. It must have sounded like any of the others just before they started off. And when I got up to leave the table
10 and said, "See you at tea time," that must have sounded all right too.

But now I don't have to do any of that. Thank Christ I don't have to do that now. I can just loosen up and let myself go. I can do or say anything I want so long as I fly this aeroplane properly. It didn't use to be like this. Four years ago it was wonderful. I loved doing it because it was exciting, because the waiting on the aerodrome was nothing more than the waiting before a football game or before going in to bat; and three years ago it was all right too. But
20 then always the three months of resting and the going back again and the resting and the going back; always going back and always getting away with it, everyone saying what a fine pilot, no one knowing what a near thing it was that time near Brussels and how lucky it was that time over Dieppe and how bad it was that other time over Dieppe and how lucky and bad and scared I've been every minute of every trip every week this year. No one knows that. They all say, "Charlie's a great pilot," "Charlie's a born flyer," "Charlie's terrific."
30   I think he was once, but not any longer.

Each time now it gets worse. At first it begins to grow upon you slowly, coming upon you slowly, creeping up on

half an hour: 30 mn □ **strap** (oneself) **in**: *se sangler*
engine: motor □ **airmen**: (airforce rank) □ **pull away the chocks**: remove the blocks that prevent the plane from moving
mine: my + noun □ **plate**: individual dish □ **in front of**: before
mouthful: quantity taken in the mouth □ **fine**: all right
Thank God: excl. of relief or gratitude □ **I'm tired of** + ing: I've had enough of □ **picking my nose** with my fingers
it must... the others: I must have given the same impression as all the other men □ **started off**: left (leave, left, left)
see you: (soon, later...) expresion of farewell □ **tea**: afternoon or evening meal

loosen up: relax
so long as: on condition that □ **fly**: pilots fly planes
properly: correctly □ **it... like this**: it was different before
ago: before now □ **wonderful**: marvellous □ **loved**: really liked
exciting: stimulating □ **the waiting**: the period of inactivity while expecting action □ **football game**: football match
bat: take one's turn at batting (= hitting the ball with a bat at cricket or baseball) □ **resting**: not flying, having a rest (= a break)

getting away with it: avoiding the accident □ **fine**: good
a near thing (it was): *je l'ai échappé belle*
Brussels: the capital of Belgium □ **lucky**: fortunate (good fortune = good luck) □ **bad**: risky, dangerous □ **over**: above
scared: frightened □ **every**: each (with no exception)
trip: flight (here), journey
great: excellent □ (he's) **a born flyer**: he's good at flying, it's a natural gift □ **terrific**: fantastic
once: before, in the past ; ≠ now
at first: at the beginning □ **grow** (upon you): impose itself
slowly ≠ rapidly □ **creeping up**: approaching secretly

you from behind, making no noise, so that you do not turn round and see it coming. If you saw it coming, perhaps you could stop it, but there is no warning. It creeps closer and closer, like a cat creeps closer stalking a sparrow, and then when it is right behind you, it doesn't spring like the cat would spring; it just leans forward and whispers in your ear. It touches you gently on the shoulder and whispers to you that you are young, that you have a million things to do and a million things to say, that if you are not careful you will
10 buy it, that you are almost certain to buy it sooner or later, and that when you do you will not be anything any longer; you will just be a charred corpse. It whispers to you about how your corpse will look when it is charred, how black it will be and how it will be twisted and brittle, with the face black and the fingers black and the shoes off the feet because the shoes always come off the feet when you die like that. At first it whispers to you only at night, when you are lying awake in bed at night. Then it whispers to you at odd moments during the day, when you are doing your teeth or
20 drinking a beer or when you are walking down the passage; and in the end it becomes so that you hear it all day and all night all the time.

There's Ijmuiden. Just the same as ever, with the little knob sticking out just beside it. There are the Frisians, Texel, Vlieland, Terschelling, Ameland, Juist and Norderney. I know them all. They look like bacteria under a microscope. There's the Zuider Zee, there's Holland, there's the North Sea, there's Belgium, and there's the world; there's the whole bloody world right there, with all the
30 people who aren't going to get killed and all the houses and the towns and the sea with all the fish. The fish aren't going to get killed either. I'm the only one that's going to get

behind: the back □ **noise**: sound □ **so**: in such a manner

if: (condition) □ see, **saw, seen** □ **perhaps**: possibly, maybe

warning: advance notice □ **closer**: nearer (comparative)

stalking: approaching quietly □ **sparrow**: small common bird

right: exactly □ **spring**: move suddenly upwards, jump

leans forward: bends to the front □ **whispers**: murmurs □ **ear**: organ of hearing □ **gently**: delicately □ **shoulder**: where the arm joins the body □ **young** ≠ old □ **a million things**: not of!

careful: cautious, prudent

buy it: (sl.) be killed □ **almost**: nearly □ **sooner or later**: some day, eventually

charred: burnt black □ **corpse**: dead body

look: seem, appear

twisted: distorted, deformed □ **brittle**: fragile, apt to break

fingers: extremities of the hands □ **off** ≠ on □ **feet**: 1 foot

die: perish □ **like that**: that way, in such circumstances

only: exclusively □ **at night**: during the night

lying: cf. lie, lay, lain in bed □ **odd**: curious, unexpected

doing your teeth: brushing them with a toothbrush and some toothpaste □ **drinking**: drink, drank, drunk (a liquid)

in the end: finally □ **all day**: not the!

all the time: incessantly

the same as ever: unchanged

knob... beside it: protuberance on its side □ **the Frisians**: a chain of islands along the coasts of Holland and Germany

them all: all of them □ **look like**: resemble □ **bacteria**: sing. bacterium □ **Zee**: Dutch word for "sea"

world: universe

whole: entire □ **bloody**: slang word used with a noun or adjective (emphatic)

towns are smaller than cities □ **sea**: ocean □ **fish**: note the plural "fish" (sometimes "fishes")

killed. I don't want to die. Oh God, I don't want to die.
I don't want to die today anyway. And it isn't the pain.
Really it isn't the pain. I don't mind having my leg mashed
or my arm burnt off; I swear to you that I don't mind that.
But I don't want to die. Four years ago I didn't mind. I
remember distinctly not minding about it four years ago. I
didn't mind about it three years ago either. It was all fine
and exciting; it always is when it looks as though you may
be going to lose, as it did then. It is always fine to fight when
10 you are going to lose everything anyway, and that was how
it was four years ago. But now we're going to win. It is so
different when you are going to win. If I die now I lose fifty
years of life, and I don't want to lose that. I'll lose anything
except that because that would be all the things I want to
do and all the things I want to see; all the things like going
on sleeping with Joey. Like going home sometimes. Like
walking through a wood. Like pouring out a drink from a
bottle. Like looking forward to week ends and like being
alive every hour every day every year for fifty years. If I die
20 now I will miss all that, and I will miss everything else. I will
miss the things that I don't know about. I think those are
really the things I am frightened of missing. I think the
reason I do not want to die is because of the things I hope
will happen. Yes, that's right. I'm sure that's right. Point a
revolver at a tramp, at a wet shivering tramp on the side of
the road and say, "I'm going to shoot you," and he will cry,
"Don't shoot. Please don't shoot." The tramp clings to life
because of the things he hopes will happen. I am clinging
to it for the same reason; but I have clung for so long now
30 that I cannot hold on much longer. Soon I will have to let
go. It is like hanging over the edge of a cliff, that's what it
is like; and I've been hanging on too long now, holding on

54

I don't want to die (or get killed): I want to live
anyway: in any case □ **pain**: suffering
I don't mind + ing: I don't object to + ing □ **mashed**: crushed
burnt off: ruined by fire □ **swear**: declare, assert

remember: recall (a past event or feeling); I remember being carefree four years ago
it looks as though: it seems that □ **may**: (possibility)
lose, lost, lost ≠ win, won, won □ **fight** a battle, the war...

so + adjective: very (intensifier)

life ≠ death; **alive** ≠ dead □ **I'll ...**: I'm willing to + verb
except: apart from, other than
like: such as □ **going on** + ing: continuing to...
sleeping with: having sexual intercourse with
through: across □ **wood**: place where trees grow □ **pouring out** or serving **from a bottle** into a glass □ **looking forward to** (sth.): waiting for sth. impatiently (pleasurable anticipation)
miss: not take advantage of □ **everything else**: all the other things

the reason (why): "why" is omitted
hope: expect and desire
happen: take place □ **that's right**: that's it
a tramp has no home, no job... □ **wet** (with rain) □ **shivering**: trembling (with cold) □ **shoot**: kill (with a firearm) □ **cry**: shout
clings to life: holds on to life, refuses to die

same: identical □ **clung**: cling, clang, clung
soon: before long □ **have to**: be forced to □ **let go**: *lâcher prise*
hanging: being suspended □ **edge**: limit □ **cliff**: high vertical rock face overhanging the sea; the white cliffs of Dover

to the top of the cliff with my fingers, not being able to pull myself back up, with my fingers getting more and more tired, beginning to hurt and to ache, so that I know that sooner or later I will have to let go. I dare not cry out for help; that is one thing that I dare not do; so I go on hanging over the side of this cliff, and as I hang I keep kicking a little with my feet against the side of the cliff, trying desperately to find a foothold, but it is steep and smooth like the side of a ship, and there isn't any foothold. I am kicking now, that's what I am doing. I am kicking against the smooth side of the cliff, and there isn't any foothold. Soon I shall have to let go. The longer I hang on the more certain I am of that, and so each hour, each day, each night, each week, I become more and more frightened. Four years ago I wasn't hanging over the edge like this. I was running about in the field above, and although I knew that there was a cliff somewhere and that I might fall over it, I did not mind. Three years ago it was the same, but now it is different.

I know that I am not a coward. I am certain of that. I will always keep going. Here I am today, at two o'clock in the afternoon, sitting here flying a course of one hundred and thirty-five at three hundred and sixty miles an hour and flying well; and although I am so frightened that I can hardly think, yet I am going on to do this thing. There was never any question of not going or of turning back. I would rather die than turn back. Turning back never enters into it. It would be easier if it did. I would prefer to have to fight that than to have to fight this fear.

There's Wassalt. Little camouflaged group of buildings and great big camouflaged aerodrome, probably full of one-o-nines and one-nineties. Holland looks wonderful. It must be a lovely place in the summer. I expect they are

coward = lâche

top ≠ bottom □ **able to**: capable of + ing □ **pull...**: haul...
more and more: increasingly
tired: weak □ **hurt and ache**: be painful (cf. p. 55, l. 2)
I dare not + infinitive without to: *je n'ose pas* □ **cry out for help**:
call out for assistance □ **go on** + ing: continue to...
side: edge □ **I keep kicking**: I repeatedly hit with my foot
trying: attempting □ **desperately**: hopelessly
foothold: place to put the foot □ **steep**: abrupt □ **smooth**: without
irregularities ; ≠ rough □ **ship**: large boat

the longer... the more certain: double comparative used to express
progression

running about: running freely □ **field**: grassland, meadow, (also)
enclosed piece of land for animals or crops □ **although**: though,
in spite of the fact that □ **might**: (possibility)

a coward is afraid to face danger, he lacks courage ; ≠ a hero
... keep going: I'll never stop, I'll never give up
course: route, direction ; the course of a ship, a river...
miles an hour or per hour: (measure of speed) 1 mile = 1.609 m

hardly: only with difficulty, almost not ; I could hardly believe it !
□ **yet**: in spite of that, even so, nevertheless □ **would rather**: would
prefer to ; I'd rather walk than run □ **... enters into it**: I never think
of going back □ **easier**: (comparative) less difficult □ **fight**: battle
against □ **fear**: strong feeling of anxiety caused by impending
danger □ **building(s)**: structure with a roof and walls (house, etc.)
full of: filled with ; ≠ empty
one-o-nines (109 s) **and one-nineties** (190 s): German aircraft
lovely: nice □ **summer**: comes before autumn □ **expect**: suppose

haymaking down there now. I expect the German soldiers are watching the Dutch girls haymaking. Bastards. Watching them haymaking, then making them come home with them afterwards. I would like to be haymaking now. I would like to be haymaking and drinking cider.

action

⌜The pilot was sitting upright in the cockpit. His face was nearly hidden by his goggles and by his oxygen mask. His right hand was resting lightly upon the stick, and his left
10 hand was forward on the throttle. All the time he was looking around him into the sky. From force of habit his head never ceased to move from one side to the other, slowly, mechanically, like clockwork, so that each moment almost, he searched every part of the blue sky, above, below and all around. But it was into the light of the sun itself that he looked twice as long as he looked anywhere else; for that is the place where the enemy hides and waits before he jumps upon you. There are only two places in which you can hide yourself when you are up in the sky. One is in cloud
20 and the other is in the light of the sun.

He flew on; and although his mind was working upon many things and although his brain was the brain of a frightened man, yet his instinct was the instinct of a pilot who is in the sky of the enemy. With a quick glance, without stopping the movement of his head, he looked down and checked his instruments. The glance took no more than a second, and like a camera can record a dozen things at once with the opening of a shutter, so he at a glance recorded with his eyes his oil pressure, his petrol, his oxygen, his rev
30 counter, boost and his air-speed, and in the same instant almost he was looking up again into the sky. He looked at the sun, and as he looked, as he screwed up his eyes and

58

haymaking: cutting and drying grass in the sun
watching: observing □ **Dutch**: of Holland □ **bastard(s)**: strong insult
afterwards: later □ **I would like to be**: I wish I were
cider: alcoholic drink made from apples

upright: straight, vertical □ **cockpit**: the pilot's compartment
hidden: made invisible (cf. hide) □ **goggles** protect the eyes
resting lightly upon: gently touching □ **stick**: *manche à balai*
forward: towards the front □ **throttle**: *manette des gaz*
around him: in all directions
ceased: stopped □ **from one side to the other**: from left to right
like clockwork: with perfect regularity
searched: examined, scrutinized □ **above**: ≠ below, under
light: (of the sun, of a lamp, of a fire...)
twice: two times, doubly □ **for**: because
hides: places himself so as not to be seen; hide, hid, hidden
jumps upon: attacks

flew on: continued to fly; fly, flew, flown □ **his mind... things**: he was busy thinking about several things □ **brain**: mind, intellect

quick glance: brief look; glance at sth. or sb.

checked: inspected, verified
record: store up □ **a dozen things**: (not of!) □ **at once**: simultaneously □ **shutter**: *obturateur (Photo)* □ **recorded**: noted
oil: lubricating liquid □ **petrol**: fuel for the engine □ **rev counter**; **boost**; **air-speed**: *compte-tours; manomètre de pression; badin (indicateur de vitesse relative)*
as: when, while □ **screwed up**: half-closed

searched into the dazzling brightness of the sun, he thought that he saw something. Yes, there it was; a small black speck moving slowly across the bright surface of the sun, and to him the speck was not a speck but a life-size German pilot sitting in a Focke Wulf which had cannon in its wings.

He knew that he had been seen. He was certain that the one above was watching him, taking his time, sure of being hidden in the brightness of the sun, watching the Spitfire and waiting to pounce. The man in the Spitfire did not take
10 his eye away from the small speck of black. His head was quite still now. He was watching the enemy, and as he watched, his left hand came away from the throttle and began to move delicately around the cockpit. It moved quickly and surely, touching this thing and that, switching on his reflector sight, turning his trigger button from "safe" over to "fire" and pressing gently with his thumb upon a lever which increased, ever so slightly, the pitch of the airscrew.

There was no thought in his head now save for the
20 thought of battle. He was no longer frightened or thinking of being frightened. All that was a dream, and as a sleeper who opens his eyes in the morning and forgets his dream, so this man had seen the enemy and had forgotten that he was frightened. It was always the same. It had happened a hundred times before, and now it was happening again. Suddenly, in an instant he had become cool and precise, and as he prepared himself, as he made ready his cockpit, he watched the German, waiting to see what he would do.

This man was a great pilot. He was great because when
30 the time came, whenever the moment arrived, his coolness was great and his courage was great, and more than anything else his instinct was great, greater by far than his

dazzling: bright, blinding □ **brightness**: brilliance, radiance
speck: small mark or spot
moving: changing position
life-size: having the real size (= dimensions)
cannon: (with or without an s) □ **wing(s)**: side (plane, bird, car)

taking his time: not hurrying
Spitfire: British fighter
pounce: attack; pounce on the enemy; pounce one one's prey
... his eye away from: stared at, fixed (focused) his eyes on
quite still: absolutely motionless

began: begin, began, begun + infinitive or gerund
switching on: turning on by means of a switch (button, lever)
reflector sight: *viseur* □ **trigger button**: firing button □ **"safe"**: no
danger □ **"fire"**: shoot □ **thumb**: short thick finger
increased ≠ reduced □ **ever so slightly**: only a little □ **the pitch of
the airscrew**: *le pas de l'hélice*
thought: idea □ **save for**: except, apart from
battle: fight, combat
a dream: sequence of imaginary thoughts □ **a sleeper**: someone
who sleeps □ **forgets**: doesn't remember
forgotten: forget, forgot, forgotten
happened: occured; when did it happen?
a hundred times: on many occasions; once, twice, 3 times...
cool: calm, composed; keep cool! (fam.)
made ready: prepared; make, made, made

whenever: every time that □ **coolness**: calmness, composure, self-
control □ **courage**: bravery, boldness
greater by far: much or a lot greater

61

coolness or his courage or his experience. Now he eased
open the throttle and pulled the stick gently backwards,
trying to gain height, trying to gain a little of the five-
thousand-feet advantage which the German had over him.
But there was not much time. The Focke Wulf came out of
the sun with its nose down and it came fast. The pilot saw
it coming and he kept going straight on, pretending that he
had not seen it, and all the time he was looking over his
shoulder, watching the German, waiting for the moment to
10 turn. If he turned too soon, the German would turn with
him, and he would be duck soup. If he turned too late, the
German would get him anyway provided that he could
shoot straight, and he would be duck soup then too. So he
watched and waited, turning his head and looking over his
shoulder, judging his distance; and as the German came
within range, as he was about to press his thumb upon the
trigger button, the pilot swerved. He yanked the stick hard
back and over to the left, he kicked hard with his left foot
upon the rudder-bar, and like a leaf which is caught up and
20 carried away by a gust of wind, the Spitfire flipped over on
to its side and changed direction. The pilot blacked out.

As his sight came back, as the blood drained away from
his head and from his eyes, he looked up and saw the
German fighter way ahead, turning with him, banking
hard, trying to turn tighter and tighter in order to get back
on the tail of the Spitfire. The fight was on. "Here we go,"
he said to himself. "Here we go again," and he smiled once,
quickly, because he was confident and because he had done
this so many times before and because each time he had
30 won.

The man was a beautiful pilot. But the German was good
too, and when the Spitfire applied a little flap in order to

eased open: opened slowly and carefully
pulled ≠ pushed □ **backwards**: towards the back; ≠ forwards
trying: attempting □ **gain** ≠ lose □ **height**: altitude
feet: cf. page 49, l. 4

nose: projecting front part (of a plane, car...) □ **fast**: quickly
straight on: in a straight (= direct) line □ **pretending that**: acting
as if

too soon: too early, before the appropriate time
duck soup: (sl.) very easy prey □ **too late**: after the appropriate time
get: hit □ **provided**: on the condition that

judging: estimating
within range: within shooting distance □ **about to**: ready to
swerved: turned suddenly aside □ **yanked hard**: (fam.) pulled
suddenly and vigorously □ **the left** ≠ the right
rudder-bar: bar that gives the direction □ **leaf**: (from a tree)
gust of wind: strong rush of air □ **flipped over**: turned over
side: left or right side □ **blacked out**: could no longer see
sight: vision □ **blood**: red liquid in the body □ **drained away**:
flowed away gradually
way ahead: far in front □ **banking**: tipping laterally
tighter and tighter: at smaller and smaller angles
tail: back end; ≠ nose □ **was on**: had started □ **here we go**: let's
go □ **smiled**: had a smile (= happy expression) on his face
confident: self-assured, undoubtful; ≠ apprehensive

beautiful: (here) good; (usually) nice to look at
flap: movement of the wing □ **in order to**: (purpose, intention)

turn in tighter circles, the Focke Wulf appeared to do the same, and they turned together. When the Spitfire throttled back suddenly and got on his tail, the Focke Wulf half-rolled and dived out and under and was away, pulling up again in a loop and rolling off the top, so that he came in again from behind. The Spitfire half-rolled and dived away, but the Focke Wulf anticipated him, and half-rolled and dived with him, behind him on his tail, and here he took a quick shot at the Spitfire, but he missed. For at least fifteen

10 minutes the two small aircraft rolled and dived around each other in the sky. Sometimes they would separate, wheeling around and around in tight turns, watching one another, circling and watching like two boxers circling each other in the ring, waiting for an opening or for the dropping of a guard; then there would be a stall-turn and one would attack the other, and the diving and the rolling and the zooming would start all over again.

All the time the pilot of the Spitfire sat upright in his cockpit, and he flew his aircraft not with his hands but with

20 the tips of his fingers, and the Spitfire was not a Spitfire but a part of his own body; the muscles of his arms and legs were in the wings and in the tail of the machine so that when he banked and turned and dived and climbed he was not moving his hands and his legs, but only the wings and the tail and the body of the aeroplane; for the body of the Spitfire was the body of the pilot, and there was no difference between the one and the other.

So it went on, and all the while, as they fought and as they flew, they lost height, coming down nearer and nearer to the

30 fields of Holland, so that soon they were fighting only three thousand feet above the ground, and one could see the hedges and the small trees and shadows which the small

appeared : seemed

together : simultaneously, jointly

half-rolled : turned upside down

dived : plunged suddenly downwards

loop : circle, curve □ **rolling off the top :** dropping down from the top (the figure described here is called "looping the loop", « *faire un looping* »)

(a) **shot :** cf. to shoot □ **missed :** did not hit it □ **at least :** at the minimum □ **each other :** one another (reciprocity)

would : (repetition of sth. in the past) □ **wheeling** (around...) : flying in circles

the ring : the place where boxers fight □ **opening :** opportunity □ **the dropping of a guard :** a moment's inattention □ **stall-turn :** *virage en décrochage* (= *perte de vitesse*)

zooming : fast movement upwards □ **start all over again :** start again from the beginning

aircraft : note the plural : aircraft

tip(s) : end ; the tips of his fingers, his fingertips

arms and legs : upper and lower limbs of a human being

climbed : flew upwards ; climb a mountain, a tree, the stairs...

for : because □ **body :** note the different uses of the word : the human body ; the body of an aircraft or any vehicle

all the while : during all that time □ **fought :** cf. fight

lost height : ≠ gained height (cf. preceding page)

ground : surface of the earth □ **one :** indefinite pronoun

hedge(s) : row of bushes or trees between fields

shadow(s) : dark shape projected by intercepting light

trees made upon the grass.

Once the German tried a long shot, from a thousand yards, and the pilot of the Spitfire saw the tracer streaming past in front of the nose of his machine. Once, when they flew close past each other, he saw, for a moment, the head and shoulders of the German under the glass roof of his cockpit, the head turned towards him, with the brown helmet, the goggles, the nose and the white scarf. Once when he blacked out from a quick pull-out, the black-out lasted
10 longer than usual. It lasted maybe five seconds, and when his sight came back, he looked quickly around for the Focke Wulf and saw it half a mile away, flying straight at him on the beam, a thin inch-long black line which grew quickly, so that almost at once it was no longer an inch, but an inch and a half, then two inches, then six and then a foot. There was hardly any time. There was a second or perhaps two at the most, but it was enough because he did not have to think or to wonder what to do; he had only to allow his instinct to control his arms and his legs and the wings and the body
20 of the aeroplane. There was only one thing to do, and the Spitfire did it. It banked steeply and turned at right-angles towards the Focke Wulf, facing it and flying straight towards it for a head-on attack.

The two machines flew fast towards each other. The pilot of the Spitfire sat upright in his cockpit, and now, more than ever, the aircraft was a part of his body. His eye was upon the reflector sight, the small yellow electric-light dot which was projected up in front of the windshield, and it was upon the thinness of the Focke Wulf beyond. Quickly, precisely,
30 he moved his aircraft a little this way and that, and the yellow dot, which moved with the aircraft, danced and jerked this way and that, and then suddenly it was upon the

66

a thousand yards: 914 m (1 yard = 3 feet = 91,44 m)
tracer: bullet that leaves a trace behind it □ **streaming:** moving straight forward; a stream, a flow (of water, traffic...)
close: near
glass roof: transparent overhead structure
towards him: in his direction
helmet: protective head-covering □ **scarf:** piece of cloth worn round the neck □ **pull-out:** manœuvre after a dive □ **lasted:** continued □ **usual:** usually, generally □ **maybe:** approximately
(looked) **for:** searched for, tried to locate
half a mile away: at a distance of 800 metres (1 mile = 1.609 m)
on the beam: on the side □ **thin** ≠ thick □ **1 inch** = 2,54 cm □ **grew:** became bigger; grow, grew, grown
a foot: 12 inches

at the most: at the maximum □ **enough:** sufficient (formal)
wonder: ask himself □ **allow:** let; allow sb. to do sth.

steeply: sharply □ **at right-angles:** at 90-degree angles

head-on: frontal, face to face (a head-on collision or crash)

(more than) **ever:** more than (ever) before

dot: round mark or spot
windshield (Am.) or windscreen: curved piece of glass at the front of a vehicle □ **the thinness:** cf. thin, 1. 13 □ **beyond:** further on
this way and that: in one direction and then in the other

jerked: moved with jerks (= sudden sharp movements)

thin line of the Focke Wulf and there it stayed. His right thumb in the leather glove felt for the firing-button; he squeezed it gently, as a rifleman squeezes a trigger, his guns fired, and at the same time, he saw the small spurts of flame from the cannon in the nose of the Focke Wulf. The whole thing, from beginning to end, took perhaps as long as it would take you to light a cigarette. The German pilot came straight on at him and he had a sudden, vivid, colourless view of the round nose and the thin outstretched wings of

10 the Focke Wulf. Then there was a crack as their wing-tips met, and there was a splintering as the port wing of the Spitfire came away from the body of the machine.

The Spitfire was dead. It fell like a dead bird falls, fluttering a little as it died; continuing in the direction of its flight as it fell. The hands of the pilot, almost in a single movement, undid his straps, tore off his helmet and slid back the hood of the cockpit; then they grasped the edges of the cockpit and he was out and away, falling, reaching for the ripcord, grasping it with his right hand, pulling on

20 it so that his parachute billowed out and opened and the straps jerked him hard between the fork of his legs.

All of a sudden the silence was great. The wind was blowing on his face and in his hair and he reached up a hand and brushed the hair away from his eyes. He was about a thousand feet up, and he looked down and saw flat green country with fields and hedges and no trees. He could see some cows in the field below him. Then he looked up, and as he looked, he said "Good God," and his right hand moved quickly to his right hip, feeling for his revolver which

30 he had not brought with him. For there, not more than five hundred yards away, parachuting down at the same time and at the same height, was another man, and he knew

stayed: stopped and remained
leather glove: *gant de cuir* □ **felt for**: tried to touch; cf. feel
squeezed: pressed □ **rifleman**: soldier with a rifle □ **trigger**: *gâchette* □ ... **fired**: he fired, he shot □ **spurt(s)**: jet

took: take, took, taken (time) □ **as long as**: the same time as
light (lit, lit) a cigarette with a lighter or a match
vivid: bright, intense □ **colourless**: without colour
view: vision □ **outstretched**: spread out, stretched out
crack: sudden sharp sound □ **wing-tips**: cf. fingertips
met: came into contact □ **splintering**: break □ **port**: left; ≠ starboard (aircraft, ship) □ **came away from**: separated from
dead: destroyed □ **fell**: came down; fall, fell, fallen
fluttering: making little quick movements, trying to fly
a single (movement): only one
... straps: *enleva ses sangles* □ **tore off**: pulled out □ **slid** (back): moved back □ **hood**: glass top □ **grasped the edges**: seized the sides
reaching for: extending his hand to catch
ripcord: cord that opens a parachute when pulled
billowed out: swelled (out) like a sail in the wind
fork: shape made by sth. that divides in two or more branches
all of a sudden: suddenly
blowing: blow, blew, blown
brushed (away): removed with his hand (as if with a brush)
flat: level, plane; ≠ hilly, mountainous
country: land in a rural area (away from towns)
cows graze in fields and produce milk □ **below**: under
"Good God": exclamation of surprise and fear
hip: upper part of the leg where it joins the body
brought: taken; bring, brought, brought

when he saw him that it could be only the German pilot. Obviously his plane had been damaged at the same time as the Spitfire in the collision. He must have got out quickly too; and now here they were, both of them parachuting down so close to each other that they might even land in the same field.

He looked again at the German, hanging there in his straps with his legs apart, his hands above his head grasping the cords of the parachute. He seemed to be a small man,
10 thickly built and by no means young. The German was looking at him too. He kept looking, and when his body swung around the other way, he turned his head, looking over his shoulder.

So they went on down. Both men were watching each other, thinking about what would happen soon, and the German was the king because he was landing in his own territory. The pilot of the Spitfire was coming down in enemy country; he would be taken prisoner, or he would be killed, or he would kill the German, and if he did that, he
20 would escape anyway, he thought. I'm sure I can run faster than the German. He does not look as though he could run very fast. I will race him across the fields and get away.

The ground was close now. There were not many seconds to go. He saw that the German would almost certainly land in the same field as he, the field with the cows. He looked down to see what the field was like and whether the hedges were thick and whether there was a gate in the hedge, and as he looked, he saw below him in the field a small pond,
30 and there was a small stream running through the pond. It was a cow-drinking pond, muddy round the edges and muddy in the water. The pond was right below him. He was

70

obviously: apparently, evidently; it's obvious that... □ **damaged**: deteriorated; smoking can damage your health □ **collision**: crash; the two planes collided or crashed into each other □ **both of them**: the two of them □ **land**: come down from the air onto the earth

apart: separated; in South Africa, black people and white people live apart (Apartheid)
thickly built: muscular □ **by no means**: not at all □ **young** ≠ old
kept: keep, kept, kept (on) + ing: continued to
swung around: turned round; swing, swung, swung

was the king: had the advantage; king, monarch □ **own**: used to emphasize the idea of possession
country: land belonging to a nation

escape: get away; escape from danger □ think, **thought**, thought
he does not look... (very fast): I don't think he can run very quickly
race him: try to beat him at running

(many seconds) to go: (many seconds) left

was like: looked like; what's it like? □ **whether**: if
thick: dense □ **gate**: passage
pond: small area of still water; duck pond, fishpond...
stream: small river, brook
muddy: covered with mud (= soft wet earth or soil)
right: exactly.

71

no more than the height of a horse above it and he was dropping fast; he was dropping right into the middle of the pond. Quickly he grasped the cords above his head and tried to spill the parachute to one side so that he would change direction, but he was too late; it wasn't any good. All at once something brushed the surface of his brain and the top of his stomach, and the fear which he had forgotten in the fighting was upon him again. He saw the pond and the black surface of the water of the pond, and the pond was
10 not a pond, and the water was not water; it was a small black hole in the surface of the earth which went on down and down for miles and miles, with steep smooth sides like the sides of a ship, and it was so deep that when you fell into it, you went on falling and falling and you fell for ever. He saw the mouth of the hole and the deepness of it, and he was only a small brown pebble which someone had picked up and thrown into the air so that it would fall into the hole. He was a pebble which someone had picked up in the grass of the field. That was all he was and now he was falling and
20 the hole was below him.

Splash. He hit the water. He went through the water and his feet hit the bottom of the pond. They sank into the mud on the bottom and his head went under the water, but it came up again and he was standing with the water up to his shoulders. The parachute was on top of him; his head was tangled in a mass of cords and white silk and he pulled at them with his hands, first this way and then that, but it only got worse, and the fear got worse because the white silk was covering his head so that he could see nothing but a mass
30 of white cloth and a tangle of cords. Then he tried to move towards the bank, but his feet were stuck in the mud; he had sunk up to his knees in the mud. So he fought the parachute

72

dropping: coming down, falling

spill: (here) tilt, tip; (also) pour out accidentally; she spilt wine all over the table (spill, spilt, spilt)
brushed... brain: passed through his mind (his head)
stomach: organ of digestion; abdomen, belly □ **forgotten**: forget, forgot, forgotten □ **(the fear) was upon him again**: he was seized with fear (he became frightened) again

hole: cavity; the men are digging a hole in the road

deep: going far down from the top
for ever: endlessly, everlastingly; I'll love you forever!
mouth: opening □ **deepness**: depth; cf. deep, 1. 13
pebble: small smooth rounded stone □ **picked up**: (from the ground) □ **thrown**: throw, threw, thrown

splash: (onomatopoeia) □ **hit**: came into violent contact with
bottom ≠ top, surface □ **sank**: went down; sink, sank, sunk

on top of him: over him, covering him
tangled: caught, trapped □ **silk**: cloth made from a fibre produced by a silkworm to make its cocoon (parachutes are made of this)

but: except
cloth: material, fabric
bank: side, edge (of a river, a lake, a pool) □ **stuck**: caught; cf. stick
knee(s): middle joint of the leg

73

and the tangled cords of the parachute, pulling at them with his hands and trying to get them clear of his head; and as he did so he heard the sound of footsteps running on the grass. He heard the noise of the footsteps coming closer and the German must have jumped, because there was a splash and he was knocked over by the weight of a man's body.

He was under the water, and instinctively he began to struggle. But his feet were still stuck in the mud, the man was on top of him and there were hands around his neck
10 holding him under and squeezing his neck with strong fingers. He opened his eyes and saw brown water. He noticed the bubbles in the water, small bright bubbles rising slowly upward in the brown water. There was no noise or shouting or anything else, but only the bright bubbles moving upward in the water, and suddenly, as he watched them, his mind became clear and calm like a sunny day. I won't struggle, he thought. There is no point in struggling, for when there is a black cloud in the sky, it is bound to rain.

20   He relaxed his body and all the muscles in his body because he had no further wish to struggle. How nice it is not to struggle, he thought. There is no point in struggling. I was a fool to have struggled so much and for so long; I was a fool to have prayed for the sun when there was a black cloud in the sky. I should have prayed for rain; I should have shouted for rain. I should have shouted, Let it rain, let it rain in solid sheets and I will not care. Then it would have been easy. It would have been so easy then. I have struggled for five years and now I don't have to do it any more. This
30 is so much better; this is ever so much better, because there is a wood somewhere that I wish to walk through, and you cannot walk struggling through a wood. There is a girl

74

tangled: mixed up, twisted
clear of: off, away from
heard: hear, heard, heard □ **(sound of) footsteps**: noise made by feet when walking

knocked over or down: hit so that he fell to the ground □ **weight**: grams, kilos, pounds are measures of weight □ **began**: begin, began, begun + infinitive or gerund □ **struggle**: fight, make great efforts; struggle against sb. or sth. □ **neck**: part of the body that joins the head to the shoulders □ **squeezing his neck...**: trying to strangle him
noticed: saw □ there are **bubbles** in champagne □ **rising**: going up; rise, rose, risen

sunny: cf. rainy; windy; cloudy; foggy...
there is no point in + ing: it's no use, there's no advantage in
it is bound to (rain): it is certain to rain

no further: no more □ **how** + adjective: exclamation
not (to struggle): "not" before the infinitive in the negative
a fool: stupid; ≠ wise, sensible
prayed for: hoped very strongly for
I should have...: used to express regret
let it rain: expression of a wish or command
rain in solid sheets: rain heavily, pour down □ **I will not care**: I won't mind, it won't matter to me

ever so much: used to emphasize the comparative "better" (comparative of "good")
cannot: often abbreviated to "can't"

somewhere that I wish to sleep with, and you cannot sleep struggling with a girl. You cannot do anything struggling; especially you cannot live struggling, and so now I am going to do all the things that I want to do, and there will be no more struggling.

See how calm and lovely it is like this. See how sunny it is and what a beautiful field this is, with the cows and the little pond and the green hedges with primroses growing in the hedges. Nothing will worry me any more now, nothing
10 nothing nothing; not even that man splashing in the water of the pond over there. He seems very puffed and out of breath. He seems to be dragging something out of the pond, something heavy. Now he's got it to the side and he's pulling it up on to the grass. How funny; it's a body. It's a body of a man. As a matter of fact, I think it's me. Yes, it is me. I know it is because of that smudge of yellow paint on the front of my flying suit. Now he's kneeling down, searching in my pockets, taking out my money and my identification card. He's found my pipe and the letter I got this morning
20 from my mother. He's taking off my watch. Now he's getting up. He's going away. He's going to leave my body behind, lying on the grass beside the pond. He's walking quickly away across the field towards the gate. How wet and excited he looks. He ought to relax a bit. He ought to relax like me. He can't be enjoying himself that way. I think I will tell him.

"Why don't you relax a bit?"

Goodness; how he jumped when I spoke to him. And his face; just look at his face. I've never seen a man look as
30 frightened as that. He's starting to run. He keeps looking back over his shoulder, but he keeps on running. But just look at his face; just look how unhappy and frightened he

especially: above all, more than anything else

what a + noun: exclamation
primrose(s): wild plant that produces pale yellow flowers in the spring □ **worry me**: make me anxious
splashing: moving noisily (in water)
puffed (fam.) = **out of breath**: breathless, breathing with difficulty
dragging: pulling along with great effort
heavy: of great weight, difficult to move
funny: surprising, strange
as a matter of fact: in fact
smudge: mark, spot □ **paint**: colouring matter
flying suit: a pilot's costume □ **kneeling down**: going down on his knees (cf. page 73, 1.32)
found: find, found, found □ **got**: get (a letter), receive
watch: small clock usually worn on the wrist
leave (behind): abandon
lying: stretched out; cf. to lie □ **beside**: near, next to, by
gate: movable barrier □ **wet**: impregnated with water; ≠ dry
ought to: should (advice) □ **a bit**: (fam.) a little
he can't be... that way: I am sure he isn't happy, excited as he is
tell, told, told, sb. sth. or sth. to sb.
why don't you...? (suggestion)
Goodness: (exclamation) My Goodness, My God □ speak, **spoke**, spoken

unhappy: miserable, sad

is. I do not want to go with him. I think I'll leave him. I think I'll stay here for a bit. I think I'll go along the hedges and find some primroses, and if I am lucky I may find some white violets. Then I will go to sleep. I will go to sleep in the sun.

I'll stay here: I won't move □ **for a bit:** for a while
lucky: fortunate
go to sleep: fall asleep; in the evening you go to bed and then you
go to sleep; be asleep = be sleeping

Grammaire au fil des nouvelles

Traduisez les phrases suivantes inspirées du texte (le premier chiffre renvoie aux pages, les suivants aux lignes) :

Maintenant que je suis seul je n'ai pas besoin de le cacher (absence d'obligation : *don't have to*..., 48 - 2).

Donc cela n'était rien *non plus* (composés de *some, any* et *no*, 48 - 28).

Ce n'était pas comme cela autrefois (forme fréquentative). **Il y a quatre ans c'était merveilleux** (50 - 15,16).

Chaque fois maintenant cela devient pire (comparatif de *bad*, 50 - 31).

Ça se rapproche (traduire *it creeps*) **de plus en plus près** (double comparatif, 52 - 3,4).

Je n'ose pas crier au secours ; c'est une chose que je n'ose pas faire (*dare, daren't*..., 56 - 4,5).

Ça doit être un endroit merveilleux l'été (supposition : *must*, 56 - 31,32).

J'aimerais être en train de faire les foins et de boire du cidre (souhait : *would like to*..., 58 - 5).

Mais il n'y avait pas beaucoup le temps (quantité imprécise, 62 - 5).

Alors qu'*il était sur le point* d'appuyer avec son pouce sur le bouton de tir... (futur imminent, 62 - 16,17).

***On* voyait les haies et les arbustes** (= petits arbres) **et les ombres *que* les arbustes faisaient sur l'herbe** (64 - 31,32 ; 66 - 1).

Les deux machines volèrent rapidement l'une vers l'autre (réciprocité, 66 - 24).

Qu'il est agréable de ne pas se battre, pensa-t-il (exclamation : *how*... ; infinitif négatif, 74 - 21,22).

J'aurais dû prier pour qu'il pleuve (= pour la pluie) (expression d'un regret : *should have* + p. passé, 74 - 25).

TASTE

"He laughs best who laughs last." (proverb).

Two men, a bottle of wine, and... a bet. A lot of suspense in this story.

There were six of us to dinner that night at Mike Schofield's house in London: Mike and his wife and daughter, my wife and I, and a man called Richard Pratt.

Richard Pratt was a famous gourmet. He was president of a small society known as the Epicures, and each month he circulated privately to its members a pamphlet on food and wines. He organized dinners where sumptuous dishes and rare wines were served. He refused to smoke for fear of harming his palate, and when discussing a wine, he had
10 a curious, rather droll habit of referring to it as though it were a living being. "A prudent wine," he would say, "rather diffident and evasive, but quite prudent." Or, "A good-humoured wine, benevolent and cheerful — slightly obscene, perhaps, but none the less good-humoured."

I had been to dinner at Mike's twice before when Richard Pratt was there, and on each occasion Mike and his wife had gone out of their way to produce a special meal for the famous gourmet. And this one, clearly, was to be no exception. The moment we entered the dining-room, I
20 could see that the table was laid for a feast. The tall candles, the yellow roses, the quantity of shining silver, the three wineglasses to each person, and above all, the faint scent of roasting meat from the kitchen brought the first warm oozings of saliva to my mouth.

As we sat down, I remembered that on both Richard Pratt's previous visits Mike had played a little betting game with him over the claret, challenging him to name its breed and its vintage. Pratt had replied that that should not be too difficult provided it was one of the great years. Mike had
30 then bet him a case of the wine in question that he could not do it. Pratt had accepted, and had won both times. Tonight I felt sure that the little game would be played over

there were six of us: note the expression (not: we were six!)

his wife: the woman to whom he was married

daughter: female child □ **and I**: not "and me"! □ **called**: named

gourmet or **epicure**: person who appreciates good food and wines

society: club □ **known as**: called □ **each month**: in January, in February... □ **pamphlet**: short publication, booklet, leaflet

dishes: food (a dish: food cooked in a particular way)

smoke (cigarettes...) □ **for fear of**: to avoid; fear, apprehension

harming: damaging □ **palate**: capacity to taste food and wine

rather: somewhat □ **droll**: odd and amusing □ **as though**: as if

were: conditional □ **living** ≠ dead □ **being**: creature □ **would**: (past habit) □ **diffident**: not assured □ **quite**: rather

benevolent: charitable □ **cheerful**: jovial □ **slightly**: a little

none the less: nevertheless, in spite of that, however

at Mike's: possessive case □ **twice**: on two occasions

had gone out of their way: had made a special effort

meal: dinner is a meal

clearly: evidently □ **was (going) to be**

entered: (rather formal) went into

laid: prepared; cf. lay □ **tall** ≠ short □ **candle(s)**: dining by candlelight is romantic! □ **shining**: bright □ **silver**: *argenterie*

above all: especially □ **faint scent**: slight smell

meat: beef, pork... □ **brought**: cf. bring □ **warm**: not hot or cold

oozing(s): flow (brought... to my mouth: made my mouth water)

sat down: sit, sat, sat at the table □ **both**: the two

previous: preceding □ **betting game**: game in which sth. valuable is risked; bet money on horses □ **claret**: red Bordeaux wine □ **breed**: type □ **vintage**: year (for wine) □ **should not be**: (probability) □ **provided**: on condition that □ **great**: reputed

won: win, won, won (a game, a bet, money...); ≠ lose, lost, lost

felt: feel, felt, felt □ **over again**: once more (repetition)

again, for Mike was quite willing to lose the bet in order to prove that his wine was good enough to be recognized, and Pratt, for his part, seemed to take a grave, restrained pleasure in displaying his knowledge.

The meal began with a plate of whitebait, fried very crisp in butter, and to go with it there was a Moselle. Mike got up and poured the wine himself, and when he sat down again, I could see that he was watching Richard Pratt. He had set the bottle in front of me so that I could read the
10 label. It said, "Geierslay Ohligsberg, 1945". He leaned over and whispered to me that Geierslay was a tiny village in the Moselle, almost unknown outside Germany. He said that this wine we were drinking was something unusual, that the output of the vineyard was so small that it was almost impossible for a stranger to get any of it. He had visited Geierslay personally the previous summer in order to obtain the few dozen bottles that they had finally allowed him to have.

"I doubt whether anyone else in the country has any of
20 it at the moment," he said. I saw him glance again at Richard Pratt. "Great thing about Moselle," he continued, raising his voice, "it's the perfect wine to serve before a claret. A lot of people serve a Rhine wine instead, but that's because they don't know any better. A Rhine wine will kill a delicate claret, you know that? It's barbaric to serve a Rhine before a claret. But a Moselle — ah! — a Moselle is exactly right."

Mike Schofield was an amiable, middle-aged man. But he was a stockbroker. To be precise, he was a jobber in the
30 stock market, and like a number of his kind, he seemed to be somewhat embarrassed, almost ashamed to find that he had made so much money with so slight a talent. In his heart

84

willing: disposed, ready □ **in order to**: so as to (purpose)

good enough: sufficiently good □ **recognized**: identified

grave: serious □ **restrained**: moderate

(take) pleasure in: enjoy □ **... knowledge**: showing what he knew

began: started □ **whitebait**: small fish □ **fried crisp**: made crunchy (or crusty) by frying

poured: served; wine is poured out of a bottle into a glass

watching: observing, looking carefully at

set: placed □ **so that**: (purpose)

label: paper stuck on the bottle □ **leaned over**: bent forward

whispered: said in a quiet voice □ **tiny**: very small

almost: nearly □ **unknown** ≠ known, famous □ **outside** ≠ in

unusual: exceptional

output: production □ **vineyard**: plantation of vines □ **small**: unimportant □ **a stranger**: someone from another place

summer: season that comes before autumn and after spring

few: serveral □ **dozen**: no "s" □ **allowed (him to have)**: let him have, sold him

I doubt...: I don't think □ **else**: other than me □ **the country**: England □ **glance (at)**: take a look at

great thing: what is interesting

raising his voice: speaking louder □ **perfect**: ideal

a lot of: many □ **instead**: in replacement

they... better: they are not expert enough □ **kill**: ruin

exactly right: perfect; right ≠ wrong

amiable: friendly □ **middle-aged**: in his fifties

strockbroker: *agent de change* □ **a jobber**: *un intermédiaire* □ **the stock market**: *la Bourse* □ **... kind**: many people in his category

somewhat: a little □ **ashamed**: very uneasy (feeling guilty)

made: earned □ **so slight a**: so little □ **in his heart**: inwardly he knew that he was not really much more than a bookmaker — an unctuous, infinitely respectable, secretly unscrupulous bookmaker — and he knew that his friends knew it, too. So he was seeking now to become a man of culture, to cultivate a literary and aesthetic taste, to collect paintings, music, books, and all the rest of it. His little sermon about Rhine wine and Moselle was a part of this thing, this culture that he sought.

"A charming little wine, don't you think?" he said. He
10 was still watching Richard Pratt. I could see him give a rapid furtive glance down the table each time he dropped his head to take a mouthful of whitebait. I could almost *feel* him waiting for the moment when Pratt would take his first sip, and look up from his glass with a smile of pleasure, of astonishment, perhaps even of wonder, and then there would be a discussion and Mike would tell him about the village of Geierslay.

But Richard Pratt did not taste his wine. He was completely engrossed in conversation with Mike's eighteen-
20 year-old daughter, Louise. He was half turned towards her, smiling at her, telling her, so far as I could gather, some story about a chef in a Paris restaurant. As he spoke, he leaned closer and closer to her, seeming in his eagerness almost to impinge upon her, and the poor girl leaned as far as she could away from him, nodding politely, rather desperately, and looking not at his face but at the topmost button of his dinner jacket.

We finished our fish, and the maid came round removing the plates. When she came to Pratt, she saw that he had not
30 yet touched his food, so she hesitated, and Pratt noticed her. He waved her away, broke off his conversation, and quickly began to eat, popping the little crisp brown fish quickly into

86

knew: was conscious that, realized; know, knew, known
a bookmaker: his job is to take bets □ **unctuous**: insincerely nice
unscrupulous: without scruples, unprincipled
seeking: trying; seek, sought, sought □ **become**: come to be
literary: note the spelling (only one "t") □ **taste**: liking
painting(s): painted picture □ **all the rest of it**: etc., and so on

sought: was looking for, was trying to find (cf. line 4)

still: expresses continuation
dropped (his head): lowered, bent
mouthful: small quantity of food taken in the mouth
sip: small quantity of drink taken in the mouth
smile of pleasure: expression of satisfaction on the face
astonishment: surprise □ **even**: (intensifier) □ **wonder**: mixture of
surprise and admiration □ **tell**, told, told

taste: test (food or wine) by taking into the mouth
engrossed: absorbed (in work, in conversation, in a book...)
year: no "s" (compound adjective) □ **half**: partly □ **towards her**:
in her direction □ **so far... gather**: I think (from what I heard)
chef: chief cook □ **as**: when, while □ speak, **spoke**, spoken
closer...: nearer... (double comparative) □ **eagerness**: ardour
impinge: impose himself □ **far** (away) ≠ near
nodding: moving her head up and down as a sign of agreement
the topmost: the highest, the uppermost
dinner jacket: a man's rather formal evening jacket, tuxedo (Am.)
maid: female servant □ **removing**: taking away
came: come, came, come □ **saw**: see, saw, seen
(not) yet: not until that moment □ **noticed**: saw
waved her away: signalled her to leave □ **broke off**: interrupted
popping: putting with a sudden movement □ **fish**: (plural)

87

his mouth with rapid jabbing movements of his fork. Then, when he had finished, he reached for his glass, and in two short swallows he tipped the wine down his throat and turned immediately to resume his conversation with Louise Schofield.

Mike saw it all. I was conscious of him sitting there, very still, containing himself, looking at his guest. His round jovial face seemed to loosen slightly and to sag, but he contained himself and was still and said nothing.

10   Soon the maid came forward with the second course. This was a large roast of beef. She placed it on the table in front of Mike who stood up and carved it, cutting the slices very thin, laying them gently on the plates for the maid to take around. When he had served everyone, including himself, he put down the carving knife and leaned forward with both hands on the edge of the table.

"Now," he said, speaking to all of us but looking at Richard Pratt. "Now for the claret. I must go and fetch the claret, if you'll excuse me."

20   "You go and fetch it, Mike?" I said. "Where is it?"

"In my study, with the cork out — breathing."

"Why the study?"

"Acquiring room temperature, of course. It's been there twenty-four hours."

"But why the study?"

"It's the best place in the house. Richard helped me choose it last time he was here."

At the sound of his name, Pratt looked round.

"That's right, isn't it?" Mike said.

30   "Yes," Pratt answered, nodding gravely. "That's right."

"On top of the green filing cabinet in my study," Mike

with... his fork: he jabbed his fork into the fish and put it quickly to his mouth □ **reached for:** moved his hand to take
swallow(s): *gorgée* □ **tipped:** poured □ **throat:** oesophagus
resume: start again, go on with

saw it all: noticed everything
still: calm □ **containing:** controlling □ a **guest** is invited
loosen and **sag:** become less happy

soon: after a short time □ **course:** a meal is usually composed of several courses
stood up: cf. stand □ **carved it:** cut it into **slices**
thin ≠ thick □ **laying:** putting □ **gently:** delicately
take around: serve
carving knife: long sharp knife used for cutting meat
edge: border, side

go and fetch: go and get, go and take ; come and see me...

study: room for work □ **cork:** bottle-stopper □ **breathing:** taking in air
of course: naturally
twenty-four hours: for (omitted) twenty-four hours

the best: superlative of "good" □ **helped:** help sb. do or to do sth.
choose, chose, chosen: make a choice
at the sound of: when he heard □ **round:** around him
right: correct, true
gravely: very seriously

on top of: above □ **a filing cabinet** is used for storing papers

said. "That's the place we chose. A good draught-free spot in a room with an even temperature. Excuse me now, will you, while I fetch it."

The thought of another wine to play with had restored his humour, and he hurried out of the door, to return a minute later more slowly, walking softly, holding in both hands a wine basket in which a dark bottle lay. The label was out of sight, facing downwards. "Now!" he cried as he came towards the table. "What about this one, Richard?
10 You'll never name this one!"

Richard Pratt turned slowly and looked up at Mike, then his eyes travelled down to the bottle nestling in its small wicker basket, and he raised his eyebrows, a slight, supercilious arching of the brows, and with it a pushing outward of the wet lower lip, suddenly imperious and ugly.

"You'll never get it," Mike said. "Not in a hundred years."

"A claret?" Richard Pratt asked, condescending.
20 "Of course."

"I assume, then, that it's from one of the smaller vineyards?"

"Maybe it is, Richard. And then again, maybe it isn't."

"But it's a good year? One of the great years?"

"Yes, I guarantee that."

"Then it shouldn't be too difficult," Richard Pratt said, drawling his words, looking exceedingly bored. Except that, to me, there was something strange about his drawling and his boredom: between the eyes a shadow of something evil,
30 and in his bearing an intentness that gave me a faint sense of uneasiness as I watched him.

"This one is really rather difficult," Mike said. "I won't

90

a draught-free spot: a place without draughts (currents of air)
even: regular, unchanging □ **will you**: equivalent of "please"

thought: idea □ **restored (his humour)**: made him happy again
hurried: rushed, ran, dashed
later: after □ **slowly** ≠ quickly □ **softly**: quietly □ **holding**:
carrying □ **basket**: container (for wine, shopping...)
out-of-sight: invisible, hidden □ **facing**: turned □ **cried**: exclaimed
towards: in the direction of

travelled: moved □ **nestling**: placed as if in a bird's nest
wicker: osier □ **raised**: lifted □ **eyebrow(s)**: line of hair above the
eye □ **supercilious**: arrogant □ **arching**: curving
... outward: forward movement □ **... lip**: *lèvre inférieure humide* □
imperious and ugly: commanding and unpleasant to look at
get it: find or guess the name of the wine □ **not...**: never

condescending: with a superior air

I assume: I suppose

maybe: perhaps □ **then again**: but then (used to introduce a
contrasting idea)

it shouldn't be: (supposition, probability)
drawling: speaking slowly □ **exceedingly bored**: extremely
uninterested
boredom: cf. bored □ **shadow**: trace □ **evil**: wicked, malevolent
bearing: attitude □ **intentness**: concentration □ **gave me...**
uneasiness: made me feel a little uncomfortable

force you to bet on this one."

"Indeed. And why not?" Again the slow arching of the brows, the cool, intent look.

"Because it's difficult."

"That's not very complimentary to me, you know."

"My dear man," Mike said, "I'll bet you with pleasure, if that's what you wish."

"It shouldn't be too hard to name it."

"You mean you want to bet?"

10 "I'm perfectly willing to bet," Richard Pratt said.

"All right, then, we'll have the usual. A case of the wine itself."

"You don't think I'll be able to name it, do you."

"As a matter of fact, and with all due respect, I don't," Mike said. He was making some effort to remain polite, but Pratt was not bothering overmuch to conceal his contempt for the whole proceeding. And yet, curiously, his next question seemed to betray a certain interest.

"You like to increase the bet?"

20 "No, Richard. A case is plenty."

"Would you like to bet fifty cases?"

"That would be silly."

Mike stood very still behind his chair at the head of the table, carefully holding the bottle in its ridiculous wicker basket. There was a trace of whiteness around his nostrils now, and his mouth was shut very tight.

Pratt was lolling back in his chair, looking up at him, the eyebrows raised, the eyes half closed, a little smile touching the corners of his lips. And again I saw, or thought I saw,

30 something distinctly disturbing about the man's face, that shadow of intentness between the eyes, and in the eyes themselves, right in their centres where it was black, a small

92

indeed: really
cool: cold, unfriendly □ **intent**: fixed

complimentary: flattering; pay sb. a compliment
my dear man: (he's condescending) □ **with pleasure**: willingly
wish: want
hard: difficult
mean, meant, meant: what does it mean?; what do you mean?
I'm perfectly willing: I'm quite ready (or happy)
all right: O.K. □ **the usual** (bet): the habitual bet

to able to: be capable of (+ ing)
as a matter of fact: in reality □ **with all due respect**: (formal) used
before expressing disagreement □ **remain**: continue to be
was not... contempt: made no effort to hide his disdain
whole: entire □ **proceeding**: course of action □ **yet**: however
betray: show, prove, be the sign of
you like: would you like □ **increase**: make bigger, raise
plenty: more than enough

silly: stupid, ridiculous
the head (of the table): the most important place at the end of the
table □ **carefully**: cautiously
whiteness: white tint □ **nostril(s)**: opening at the end of the nose
shut very tight: very firmly closed
lolling back: sitting back, relaxing
half closed: partly closed (not open, not closed)
the corners of his lips: the sides of his mouth
disturbing: troubling

right (adverb): exactly □ **their centres...**: the pupils

slow spark of shrewdness, hiding.

"So you don't want to increase the bet?"

"As far as I'm concerned, old man, I don't give a damn," Mike said. "I'll bet you anything you like."

The three women and I sat quietly, watching the two men. Mike's wife was becoming annoyed; her mouth had gone sour and I felt that at any moment she was going to interrupt. Our roast beef lay before us on our plates, slowly steaming.

10 "So you'll bet me anything I like?"

"That's what I told you. I'll bet you anything you damn well please, if you want to make an issue out of it."

"Even ten thousand pounds?"

"Certainly I will, if that's the way you want it." Mike was more confident now. He knew quite well that he could call any sum Pratt cared to mention.

"So you say I can name the bet?" Pratt asked again.

"That's what I said."

There was a pause while Pratt looked slowly around the 20 table, first at me, then at the three women, each in turn. He appeared to be reminding us that we were witnesses to the offer.

"Mike!" Mrs Schofield said, "Mike, why don't we stop this nonsense and eat our food. It's getting cold."

"But it isn't nonsense," Pratt told her evenly. "We're making a little bet."

I noticed the maid standing in the background holding a dish of vegetables, wondering whether to come forward with them or not.

30 "All right, then," Pratt said. "I'll tell you what I want you to bet."

"Come on, then," Mike said, rather reckless. "I don't give

94

spark: trace □ **shrewdness**: sagacity □ **hiding**: cf. hide (hid, hidden) conceal, keep secret

as far as...: as for me □ **I don't give a damn**: (fam.) I don't care

anything you like: what you want (or wish)

quietly: silently

annoyed: irritated, displeased

gone sour: become morose (sullen, gloomy) □ **felt**: had the impression that

steaming: giving out steam or vapour

damn well: (sl.) used for emphasis

(you) please: you want □ **make an issue...**: make a problem of it, make a fuss about it □ **even**: (intensifier)

the way you want it: how you want it, what you want

confident: self-assured □ **knew**: know, knew, known

any: no matter what □ **cared to**: wanted to

while: during which

each in turn: one after the other

appeared: seemed □ **reminding us**: making us realize □ **witness(es)**: a witness is present when sth. happens and can testify, afterwards

why don't we...: why not..., we should... (suggestion)

nonsense: stupid or foolish business □ **getting**: becoming (+ adj.)

evenly: calmly; even-tempered = calm, placid

in the background: at the back, behind

vegetable(s): potato, carrot... □ **wondering... (or not)**: asking herself (trying to decide) if she should bring the dish to the table or not □ **I want you...**: note the construction: to want sb. to do sth.

come on: tell me □ **reckless**: not afraid, daring, bold

a damn what it is — you're on."

Pratt nodded, and again the little smile moved the corners of his lips, and then, quite slowly, looking at Mike all the time, he said, "I want you to bet me the hand of your daughter in marriage."

Louise Schofield gave a jump. "Hey!" she cried. "No! That's not funny! Look here, Daddy, that's not funny at all."

"No, dear," her mother said. "They're only joking."

10 "I'm not joking," Richard Pratt said.

"It's ridiculous," Mike said. He was off balance again now.

"You said you'd bet anything I liked."

"I meant money."

"You didn't *say* money."

"That's what I meant."

"Then it's a pity you didn't say it. But anyway, if you wish to go back on your offer, that's quite all right with me."

"It's not a question of going back on my offer, old man.

20 It's a no-bet anyway, because you can't match the stake. You yourself don't happen to have a daughter to put up against mine in case you lose. And if you had, I wouldn't want to marry her."

"I'm glad of that, dear," his wife said.

"I'll put up anything you like," Pratt announced. "My house, for example. How about my house?"

"Which one? Mike asked, joking now.

"The country one."

"Why not the other one as well?"

30 "All right then, if you wish it. Both my houses."

At that point I saw Mike pause. He took a step forward and placed the bottle in its basket gently down on the table.

96

you're on: you have in mind

all the time: continuously, uninterruptedly

gave a jump (or a start): made a quick sudden movement
funny: amusing □ **look here**: used to draw sb.'s attention before speaking when angry or impatient □ **(not) at all**: (not) in any way
dear: darling (affectionate term) □ **only joking**: not speaking seriously
off balance: disconcerted, perplexed, puzzled

you'd: you would (conditional)
I meant: I was thinking of..., what I had in mind was...

it's a pity: it's unfortunate □ **anyway**: in spite of that
go back on: not keep □ **that's... with me**: I don't mind at all

match the stake: make the same offer
put up: offer
against: in exchange for □ **mine**: my daughter □ **in case**: if
marry sb.: (not "with"); ≠ divorce sb.
glad: happy, pleased

how about: what about (introducing a suggestion)
which one?: which house? ("which" is used when there is a choice)
the country one: the house that is situated in the country (≠ in town) □ **as well**: also, too, in addition

point: exact moment □ **took a step**: moved, walked (forward)

He moved the salt-cellar to one side, then the pepper, and then he picked up his knife, studied the blade thoughtfully for a moment, and put it down again. His daughter, too, had seen him pause.

"Now, Daddy!" she cried. "Don't be *absurd!* It's *too* silly for words. I refuse to be betted on like this."

"Quite right, dear," her mother said. "Stop it at once, Mike, and sit down and eat your food."

Mike ignored her. He looked over at his daughter and he
10 smiled, a slow, fatherly, protective smile. But in his eyes, suddenly, there glimmered a little triumph. "You know," he said, smiling as he spoke. "You know, Louise, we ought to think about this a bit."

"Now, stop it, Daddy! I refuse even to listen to you! Why, I've never heard anything so ridiculous in my life!"

"No, seriously, my dear. Just wait a moment and hear what I have to say."

"But I don't *want* to hear it."

"Louise! Please! It's like this. Richard, here, has offered
20 us a serious bet. He is the one who wants to make it, not me. And if he loses, he will have to hand over a considerable amount of property. Now, wait a minute, my dear, don't interrupt. The point is this. *He cannot possibly win.*"

"He seems to think he can."

"Now listen to me, because I know what I'm talking about. The expert, when tasting a claret — so long as it is not one of the famous great wines like Lafite or Latour — can only get a certain way towards naming the vineyard. He can, of course, tell you the Bordeaux district from which the
30 wine comes, whether it is from St Emilion, Pomerol, Graves, or Médoc. But then each district has several communes, little counties, and each county has many, many

98

salt-cellar: small pot for salt □ **pepper** is used to season food

picked up: took □ **knife**: cutting instrument with a metal **blade**

too silly (for words): extremely stupid; too + adj. = excessively

be betted on: (passive voice)

quite right: absolutely, I agree □ **at once**: immediately

fatherly: typical of a father □ **protective**: giving protection

there glimmered...: there was a sign of...

ought to: should (advice, suggestion); you ought to smoke less

think: reflect □ **a bit**: (fam.) a little, for a little while

why: interjection expressing impatience, annoyance

hear, heard, heard □ **(never) in my life**: never before

have to: be obliged to □ **hand over**: give (to sb. else)

amount: extent □ **property**: land and buildings

point: important idea □ **he cannot possibly win**: it is impossible that he wins

so long as or as long as: on condition that, provided

can only... vineyard: cannot name the vineyard precisely (only approximately) □ **district**: area

whether (... or...): if... or...

each: every □ **several**: some, a few

counties: England is divided into 45 counties

small vineyards. It is impossible for a man to differentiate between them all by taste and smell alone. I don't mind telling you that this one I've got here is a wine from a small vineyard that is surrounded by many other small vineyards, and he'll never get it. It's impossible."

"You can't be sure of that," his daughter said.

"I'm telling you I can. Though I say it myself, I understand quite a bit about this wine business, you know. And anyway, heavens alive, girl, I'm your father and you
10 don't think I'd let you in for — for something you didn't want, do you? I'm trying to make you some money."

"Mike!" his wife said sharply. "Stop it now, Mike, please!"

Again he ignored her. "If you will take this bet," he said to his daughter, "in ten minutes you will be the owner of two large houses."

"But I don't want two large houses, Daddy."

"Then sell them. Sell them back to him on the spot. I'll arrange all that for you. And then, just think of it, my dear,
20 you'll be rich! You'll be independent for the rest of your life!"

"Oh, Daddy, I don't like it. I think it's silly."

"So do I," the mother said. She jerked her head briskly up and down as she spoke, like a hen. "You ought to be ashamed of yourself, Michael, ever suggesting such a thing! Your own daughter, too!"

Mike didn't even look at her. "Take it!" he said eagerly, staring hard at the girl. "Take it, quick! I'll guarantee you won't lose."

30 "But I don't like it, Daddy."

"Come on, girl. Take it!"

Mike was pushing her hard. He was leaning towards her,

taste ; smell : 2 of the 5 senses □ **alone :** only □ **I don't mind... :** I'm quite happy to tell you, you must know that...
surrounded by : situated among or in the middle of
get it : find it, guess it

though : although, in spite of the fact that □ **I understand... :** I know quite a lot of things concerning wine
heavens alive : (excl.) heaven is the place where God supposedly lives □ **let you in :** get you involved

sharply : abruptly, harshly

will : decide to ("if" is not usually followed by the future)
the owner is the person who owns (= possesses) sth.
large : big (long and wide)

sell, sold, sold : exchange for money □ **on the spot :** immediately

independent : (note the spelling) □ **for the rest of your life :** forever ; life : period between birth and death

so do I : (agreement) □ **jerked :** moved, shook □ **briskly :** vigourously □ **hen :** female chicken
ashamed : cf. page 85, 1. 31 □ **such a thing :** a thing like that
own : emphasizes the idea of possession □ **too :** what's more
take it : accept it □ **eagerly :** with impatient desire
staring hard : looking fixedly and intensely □ **quick :** fast

come on : exclamation expressing encouragement
hard : strongly, firmly

fixing her with two hard bright eyes, and it was not easy for
the daughter to resist him.

"But what if I lose?"

"I keep telling you, you can't lose. I'll guarantee it."

"Oh, Daddy, must I?"

"I'm making you a fortune. So come on now. What do
you say, Louise? All right?"

For the last time, she hesitated. Then she gave a helpless
little shrug of the shoulders and said, "Oh, all right, then.
10 Just so long as you swear there's no danger of losing."

"Good!" Mike cried. "That's fine! Then it's a bet!"

"Yes," Richard Pratt said, looking at the girl. "It's a
bet."

Immediately, Mike picked up the wine, tipped the first
thimbleful into his own glass, then skipped excitedly around
the table filling up the others. Now everyone was watching
Richard Pratt, watching his face as he reached slowly for his
glass with his right hand and lifted it to his nose. The man
was about fifty years old and he did not have a pleasant face.
20 Somehow, it was all mouth — mouth and lips — the full,
wet lips of the professional gourmet, the lower lip hanging
downward in the centre, a pendulous, permanently open
taster's lip, shaped open to receive the rim of a glass or a
morsel of food. Like a keyhole, I thought, watching it; his
mouth is like a large wet keyhole.

Slowly he lifted the glass to his nose. The point of the nose
entered the glass and moved over the surface of the wine,
delicately sniffing. He swirled the wine gently around in the
glass to receive the bouquet. His concentration was intense.
30 He had closed his eyes, and now the whole top half of his
body, the head and neck and chest, seemed to become a
kind of huge sensitive smelling-machine, receiving, filtering,

102

not easy: difficult

what if: what will happen if
I keep telling you: I have repeatedly told you; keep doing sth. =
do sth. again and again □ **must I?**: do I have to? (obligation)

last ≠ first □ **helpless**: resigned
shrug of the shoulders: *haussement d'épaules*
swear: promise; swear, swore, sworn
fine: very good, perfect

thimbleful: very small quantity □ **skipped**: walked with jumping
movements □ **filling up**: pouring wine into; fill up, make full ≠
empty
lifted: raised □ **nose**: organ of smell
about: approximately □ **pleasant**: friendly
somehow: in some way, for some reason □ **full**: thick
wet lips: cf. p. 91, 1. 15 □ **lower** ≠ upper □ **hanging**: cf. hang, hung,
hung □ **pendulous**: drooping
shaped: designed □ **rim**: border, edge
morsel: small piece □ **keyhole**: opening for the key in a door

sniffing: smelling □ **swirled**: moved with twisting turns
bouquet: smell or aroma of wine
top half: upper part; top ≠ bottom
neck: between head and trunk □ **chest**: top front part of the trunk
kind: sort □ **huge**: enormous □ **sensitive**: perceptive, perceiving

analysing the message from the sniffing nose.

Mike, I noticed, was lounging in his chair, apparently unconcerned, but he was watching every move. Mrs Schofield, the wife, sat prim and upright at the other end of the table, looking straight ahead, her face tight with disapproval. The daughter, Louise, had shifted her chair away a little, and sidewise, facing the gourmet, and she, like her father, was watching closely.

For at least a minute, the smelling process continued; then, without opening his eyes or moving his head, Pratt lowered the glass to his mouth and tipped in almost half the contents. He paused, his mouth full of wine, getting the first taste; then, he permitted some of it to trickle down his throat and I saw his Adam's apple move as it passed by. But most of it he retained in his mouth. And now, without swallowing again, he drew in through his lips a thin breath of air which mingled with the fumes of the wine in the mouth and passed on down into his lungs. He held the breath, blew it out through his nose, and finally began to roll the wine around under the tongue, and chewed it, actually chewed it with his teeth as though it were bread.

It was a solemn, impressive performance, and I must say he did it well.

"Um," he said, putting down the glass, running a pink tongue over his lips. "Um — yes. A very interesting little wine — gentle and gracious, almost feminine in the after-taste."

There was an excess of saliva in his mouth, and as he spoke he spat an occasional bright speck of it on to the table.

"Now we can start to eliminate," he said. "You will pardon me for doing this carefully, but there is much at

104

analysing: to analyse; an analysis
lounging: sitting in a relaxed manner
unconcerned: uninterested □ **move**: movement, step
prim and upright: looking formal and strict
straight ahead: in front of her □ **tight**: looking severe
disapproval: reproach, disagreement □ **shifted**: moved
sidewise: to the side
closely: with attention, carefully
at least a minute: a minute or more □ **process**: operation
without + ing: not + ing; he spoke without looking at me
lowered: moved downwards
the contents: (note the "s") what the bottle contains
some: a little □ **trickle down**: go down (or flow) slowly
most: the biggest part or quantity
retained: kept, held (hold, held, held)
drew in: inhaled □ **thin breath**: small quantity (of air)
mingled: mixed □ **fumes**: emanations, smell; petrol fumes...
lung(s): breathing organ □ **blew (it) out**: exhaled; blow, blew,
blown □ **finally**: in the end, eventually
tongue: muscle in the mouth □ **actually**: really □ **chewed**: you
chew food with your **teeth** (sing. tooth); chewing-gum
solemn: ceremonious □ **impressive**: imposing □ **performance**: act,
show
pink: light red; the Pink Panther (Peter Sellers)

aftertaste: taste that stays in the mouth after the drink (or food)
has been swallowed

spit, spat, spat: eject from the mouth □ **speck**: small quantity

pardon me: excuse me, forgive me (for + ing)

105

stake. Normally I would perhaps take a bit of a chance, leaping forward quickly and landing right in the middle of the vineyard of my choice. But this time — I must move cautiously this time, must I not?" He looked up at Mike and he smiled, a thick-lipped, wet-lipped smile. Mike did not smile back.

"First, then, which district in Bordeaux does this wine come from? That's not too difficult to guess. It is far too light in the body to be from either St Emilion or Graves.
10 It is obviously a Médoc. There's no doubt about *that*.

"Now — from which commune in Médoc does it come? That also, by elimination, should not be too difficult to decide. Margaux? No. It cannot be Margaux. It has not the violent bouquet of a Margaux. Pauillac? It cannot be Pauillac, either. It is too tender, too gentle and wistful for Pauillac. The wine of Pauillac has a character that is almost imperious in its taste. And also, to me, a Pauillac contains just a little pith, a curious, dusty, pithy flavour that the grape acquires from the soil of the district. No, no. This —
20 this is a very gentle wine, demure and bashful in the first taste, emerging shyly but quite graciously in the second. A little arch, perhaps, in the second taste, and a little naughty also, teasing the tongue with a trace, just a trace of tannin. Then, in the after-taste, delightful — consoling and feminine, with a certain blithely generous quality that one associates only with the wines of the commune of St Julien. Unmistakably this is a St Julien."

He leaned back in his chair, held his hands up level with his chest, and placed the fingertips carefully together. He
30 was becoming ridiculously pompous, but I thought that some of it was deliberate, simply to mock his host. I found myself waiting rather tensely for him to go on. The girl

... stake: the bet is quite important □ **chance**: risk
leaping forward... (of my choice): giving, without hesitating, the precise name of the vineyard I had decided on
cautiously: with caution or care, carefully

guess: find out □ **far too** (+ adj.): very much, considerably
light ≠ heavy □ **either... or ...**: (two possibilities)
obviously: clearly, evidently

wistful: melancholy, nostalgic

pith: vigour □ **dusty**: earthy □ **flavour**: savour
grape: raisins are dried grapes □ **soil**: land, ground, earth
demure: modest, reserved □ **bashful**: shy, timid

arch: malicious □ **naughty**: titillating
teasing: playing with, tickling □ **tannin**: *tanin*
delightful: very pleasing; I'm delighted (= very pleased) to be here
blithely: happily

unmistakably: undoubtedly, clearly, obviously; mistake = error
level with: just in front of
fingertip(s): tip or end of the finger □ **(placed) together**: joined

deliberate: intentional □ **mock** (sb.): make fun of □ **host**: the one who invites □ **tensely**: anxiously □ **go on**: continue

107

Louise was lighting a cigarette. Pratt heard the match strike and he turned on her, flaring suddenly with real anger. "Please!" he said. "Please don't do that! It's a disgusting habit, to smoke at table!"

She looked up at him, still holding the burning match in one hand, the big slow eyes settling on his face, resting there a moment, moving away again, slow and contemptuous. She bent her head and blew out the match, but continued to hold the unlighted cigarette in her fingers.

10   "I'm sorry, my dear," Pratt said, "but I simply cannot have smoking at table."

She didn't look at him again.

"Now, let me see — where were we?" he said. "Ah, yes. This wine is from Bordeaux, from the commune of St Julien, in the district of Médoc. So far, so good. But now we come to the more difficult part — the name of the vineyard itself. For in St Julien there are many vineyards, and as our host so rightly remarked earlier on, there is often not much difference between the wine of one and the wine

20 of another. But we shall see."

He paused again, closing his eyes. "I am trying to establish the 'growth'," he said. "If I can do that, it will be half the battle. Now, let me see. This wine is obviously not from a first-growth vineyard — nor even a second. It is not a great wine. The quality, the — the — what do you call it? — the radiance, the power, is lacking. But a third growth — that it could be. And yet I doubt it. We know it is a good year — our host has said so — and this is probably flattering it a little bit. I must be careful. I must be very careful

30 here."

He picked up his glass and took another small sip.

"Yes," he said, sucking his lips, "I was right. It is a fourth

a **match** can be used for **lighting** a cigarette (you **strike** it on the matchbox) □ **flaring...** : becoming suddenly very angry

burning : lighted ; burn, burnt, burnt
settling, resting : fixed
contemptuous : disdainful, scornful
bend, **bent**, bent : inclined □ **blew out** : extinguished ; blow, blew, blown

have : accept, permit, allow ; I won't have any noise while I'm working !
let me see : I must think carefully about this

so far, so good : everything I've guessed up to now is correct

for : because
earlier on : before ; ≠ later on, after

trying : attempting
"growth" : cf. grow, grew, grown ; a vinegrowing district
... half the battle : the biggest problem will be solved
first-growth : *premier cru* ; first, second, third, fourth...
call : name ; what's it called ?, what's its name ?
radiance : brightness □ **power** : strength □ **lacking** : absent, missing
yet : however □ **I doubt it** : I don't think it is
flattering (it) : making (it) better

sucking : drawing in ; the baby sucks at its mother's breast

growth. Now I am sure of it. A fourth growth from a very good year — from a great year, in fact. And that's what made it taste for a moment like a third — or even a second-growth wine. Good! That's better! Now we are closing in! What are the fourth-growth vineyards in the commune of St Julien?"

Again he paused, took up his glass, and held the rim against that sagging, pendulous lower lip of his. Then I saw the tongue shoot out, pink and narrow, the tip of it dipping
10 into the wine, withdrawing swiftly again — a repulsive sight. When he lowered the glass, his eyes remained closed, the face concentrated, only the lips moving, sliding over each other like two pieces of wet, spongy rubber.

"There it is again!" he cried. "Tannin in the middle taste, and the quick astringent squeeze upon the tongue. Yes, yes, of course! Now I have it! The wine comes from one of those small vineyards around Beychevelle. I remember now. The Beychevelle district, and the river and the little harbour that has silted up so the wine ships can no longer use it.
20 Beychevelle... could it actually be a Beychevelle itself? No, I don't think so. Not quite. But it is somewhere very close. Château Talbot? Could it be Talbot? Yes, it could. Wait one moment."

He sipped the wine again, and out of the side of my eye I noticed Mike Schofield and how he was leaning farther and farther forward over the table, his mouth slightly open, his small eyes fixed upon Richard Pratt.

"No. I was wrong. It is not a Talbot. A Talbot comes forward to you just a little quicker than this one; the fruit
30 is nearer the surface. If it is a '34, which I believe it is, then it couldn't be Talbot. Well, well. Let me think. It is not a Beychevelle and it is not a Talbot, and yet — yet it is so close

sure of it: certain (or positive) about it

better: comparative of "good" □ **closing in**: approaching

sagging: hanging
shoot out: come out fast □ **narrow** ≠ wide □ **tip**: end □ **dipping**: plunging □ **...swiftly**: moving back fast □ **repulsive sight**: disgusting vision
sliding over each other: moving along one another
spongy: soft (like a sponge) □ **rubber**: elastic substance

astringent squeeze: bitter taste

harbour: port (place of shelter for vessels)
silted up: become filled with alluvial deposit □ **ship(s)**: large vessel (bigger than a boat) □ **actually**: really
...so: ...it is □ **quite**: exactly □ **close**: near; ≠ far

farther or further: comparative of "far"

wrong ≠ right (note the auxiliary: to be right or wrong)

a ' 34: a wine from the year 1934 □ **believe**: think

to both of them, so close, that the vineyard must be almost in between. Now, which could that be?"

He hesitated, and we waited, watching his face. Everyone, even Mike's wife, was watching him now. I heard the maid put down the dish of vegetables on the sideboard behind me, gently, so as not to disturb the silence.

"Ah!" he cried. "I have it! Yes, I think I have it!"

For the last time, he sipped the wine. Then, still holding the glass up near his mouth, he turned to Mike and he
10 smiled, a slow, silky smile, and he said, "You know what this is? This is the little Château Branaire-Ducru."

Mike sat tight, not moving.

"And the year, 1934."

We all looked at Mike, waiting for him to turn the bottle around in its basket and show the label.

"Is that your final answer?" Mike said.

"Yes, I think so."

"Well, is it or isn't it?"

"Yes, it is."

20 "What was the name again?"

"Château Branaire-Ducru. Pretty little vineyard. Lovely old château. Know it quite well. Can't think why I didn't recognize it at once."

"Come on, Daddy," the girl said. "Turn it round and let's have a peek. I want my two houses."

"Just a minute," Mike said. "Wait just a minute." He was sitting very quiet, bewildered-looking, and his face was becoming puffy and pale, as though all the force was draining slowly out of him.

30 "Michael" his wife called sharply from the other end of the table. "What's the matter?"

"Keep out of this, Margaret, will you please."

in between : in the middle

sideboard : piece of dining-room furniture with drawers, cupboards and shelves ☐ **disturb :** break (the silence)

silky : as soft as silk *(la soie)*, gentle

tight : tense ☐ **not moving :** motionless, completely still

show : allow to be seen, disclose
final : last, definite

what was the name again ? : can you repeat the name ?
pretty : lovely, nice
old : ancient ☐ **château :** castle or large country house in France

have a peek : have a quick look or glance

bewildered : confused, puzzled
puffy : swollen (cf. swell), bloated
draining (out) : flowing out ; drain, pipe through which a liquid is carried away
what's the matter ? : what's happening ? what's wrong ?
keep out of this : don't intervene, don't interfere

Richard Pratt was looking at Mike, smiling with his mouth, his eyes small and bright. Mike was not looking at anyone.

"Daddy!" the daughter cried, agonized. "But, Daddy, you don't mean to say he's guessed it right!"

"Now, stop worrying, my dear," Mike said. "There's nothing to worry about."

I think it was more to get away from his family than anything else that Mike then turned to Richard Pratt and
10 said, "I'll tell you what, Richard. I think you and I better slip off into the next room and have a little chat."

"I don't want a little chat," Pratt said. "All I want is to see the label on that bottle." He knew he was a winner now; he had the bearing, the quiet arrogance of a winner, and I could see that he was prepared to become thoroughly nasty if there was any trouble. "What are you waiting for?" he said to Mike. "Go on and turn it round."

Then this happened: the maid, the tiny, erect figure of the maid in her white-and-black uniform, was standing beside
20 Richard Pratt, holding something out in her hand. "I believe these are yours, sir," she said.

Pratt glanced around, saw the pair of thin horn-rimmed spectacles that she held out to him, and for a moment he hesitated. "Are they? Perhaps they are, I don't know."

"Yes, sir, they're yours." The maid was an elderly woman — nearer seventy than sixty — a faithful family retainer of many years' standing. She put the spectacles down on the table beside him.

Without thanking her, Pratt took them up and slipped
30 them into his top pocket, behind the white handkerchief.

But the maid didn't go away. She remained standing beside and slightly behind Richard Pratt, and there was

agonized: in agony

worrying: being anxious; worry about sth; be worried

get away from: escape from
anything else: for any other reason

slip off: move discreetly □ **next**: adjoining □ **little chat**: brief conversation
winner ≠ loser
bearing: posture, attitude, demeanour
prepared: ready □ **thoroughly**: completely □ **nasty**: malicious, unkind, mean □ **trouble**: problem
round: to the other side
happened: took place □ **erect**: upright □ **figure**: shape of the body
beside: near, next to

are yours: belong to you □ **sir**: respectful term used when addressing a man □ **horn-rimmed**: *à monture d'écaille*
(pair of) **spectacles**: formal word for (pair of) glasses

elderly: getting near old age; the elderly (collective noun)
faithful: loyal □ **family retainer of... standing**: servant who has been with the family for a long time

slipped (them): put (them) quickly
top pocket: breast pocket □ **handkerchief**: small square of material used as ornament (here) or for blowing one's nose

115

something so unusual in her manner and in the way she stood there, small, motionless and erect, that I for one found myself watching her with a sudden apprehension. Her old grey face had a frosty, determined look, the lips were compressed, the little chin was out, and the hands were clasped together tight before her. The curious cap on her head and the flash of white down the front of her uniform made her seem like some tiny, ruffled, white-breasted bird.

10   "You left them in Mr Schofield's study," she said. Her voice was unnaturally, deliberately polite. "On top of the green filing cabinet in his study, sir, when you happened to go in there by yourself before dinner."

It took a few moments for the full meaning of her words to penetrate, and in the silence that followed I became aware of Mike and how he was slowly drawing himself up in his chair, and the colour coming to his face, and the eyes opening wide, and the curl of the mouth, and the dangerous little patch of whiteness beginning to spread around the area

20   of the nostrils.

"Now, Michael!" his wife said. "Keep calm now, Michael, dear! Keep calm!"

manner: behaviour; a good-mannered (≠ bad-mannered) child
I for one: I myself, I personally

grey: pale □ **frosty**: very cold, unfriendly
chin: part of the face below the mouth; a pointed chin
clasped together: joined □ **cap**: head-covering
flash of white: streak of white colour
some: a sort of □ **ruffled**: *ébouriffé* □ **white-breasted (bird)**: the penguin is a white-breasted bird
left: forgot; leave, left, left sth. somewhere

by yourself: alone, unaccompanied
it took... (penetrate): a short time elapsed before we realized the implications of what she had said □ **followed**: came afterwards □ **(became) aware of**: noticed

wide: completely; wide-open mouth, door... □ **curl**: contraction
patch of whiteness: spot of white colour □ **spread**: get bigger, stretch out; spread (spread, spread) butter on bread
keep calm!: don't get excited!, take it easy!

Grammaire au fil des nouvelles

Traduisez les phrases suivantes inspirées du texte (le premier chiffre renvoie aux pages, les suivants aux lignes):

Nous étions six à dîner ce soir-là chez Mike Schofield à Londres : Mike, sa femme et sa fille, ma femme et moi, et un homme nommé Richard Pratt (82 - 1,2,3).

Pratt avait répondu que cela ne devrait pas être trop difficile (probabilité : *should...*, 82 - 28,29).

La production du vignoble était si petite qu'il était presque impossible pour un étranger de s'en procurer (si... que ; quantité indéfinie : *some, any, no* (84 - 14,15).

Je dois aller chercher le Bordeaux (auxiliaire modal *must ; go and...*, 88 - 18).

C'est le meilleur endroit de la maison (superlatif de *good* ; préposition après un superlatif, 88 - 26).

Mike, pourquoi n'arrêtons-nous pas ces bêtises et ne mangeons-nous pas notre nourriture ? (suggestion : *why...?*, 94 - 23,24).

Je veux que vous pariiez (avec moi) la main de votre fille en mariage (proposition infinitive après *to want*, 96 - 4,5).

Je refuse que l'on parie ainsi sur moi (voix passive, 98 - 6).

Je n'ai jamais rien entendu d'aussi ridicule de toute ma vie (*never + p. perfect* ; composés de *some, any, no* ; *so* + adj., 98 - 15).

Je pense que c'est stupide. Moi aussi (100 - 22,23).

Tu devrais avoir honte de toi, Michael (100 - 24,25).

De quelle région du Bordelais (traduire : de Bordeaux) **ce vin vient-il ?** (question pour un choix restreint ; rejet de la préposition, 106 - 7,8).

Car à St Julien il y a beaucoup de vignobles... (quantité imprécise, 108 - 17).

Maintenant j'en suis sûr (110 - 1).

THE WAY UP TO HEAVEN

While his wife was getting ready to go to Paris for three weeks, little did Mr. Foster know that he would also go on a long journey, all by himself.

All her life, Mrs. Foster had had an almost pathological fear of missing a train, a plane, a boat, or even a theatre curtain. In other respects, she was not a particularly nervous woman, but the mere thought of being late on occasions like these would throw her into such a state of nerves that she would begin to twitch. It was nothing much — just a tiny vellicating muscle in the corner of the left eye, like a secret wink — but the annoying thing was that it refused to disappear until an hour or so after the train or plane or
10 whatever it was had been safely caught.

It was really extraordinary how in certain people a simple apprehension about a thing like catching a train can grow into a serious obsession. At least half an hour before it was time to leave the house for the station, Mrs. Foster would step out of the elevator all ready to go, with hat and coat and gloves, and then, being quite unable to sit down, she would flutter and fidget about from room to room until her husband, who must have been well aware of her state, finally emerged from his privacy and suggested in a cool dry
20 voice that perhaps they had better get going now, had they not?

Mr. Foster may possibly have had a right to be irritated by this foolishness of his wife's, but he could have had no excuse for increasing her misery by keeping her waiting unnecessarily. Mind you, it is by no means certain that this is what he did, yet whenever they were to go somewhere, his timing was so accurate — just a minute or two late, you understand — and his manner so bland that it was hard to believe he wasn't purposely inflicting a nasty private little
30 torture of his own on the unhappy lady. And one thing he must have known — that she would never dare to call out and tell him to hurry. He had disciplined her too well for

all her life: always □ **almost**: nearly
fear: apprehension □ **missing**: being too late to catch
... curtain: the start of a performance □ **in other respects**: otherwise
the mere thought: just the idea □ **late**: not in time
would: (past habit) □ **throw... nerves**: make her feel so nervous
twitch: contract spasmodically □ **tiny**: very small
vellicating: twitching □ **left** ≠ right
wink: closing and opening of the eye □ **annoying**: irritating
disappear: stop □ **until**: before □ **or so**: approximately
(the train...) caught: she was on board the train, the plane or any
other means of transport; catch, caught, caught
grow (into): become, develop into
serious: important □ **at least...**: not less than 30 minutes
leave: go away from □ **station**: railway station; bus station
step out: come out □ **elevator** (Am.): lift □ **ready**: prepared
gloves (for hands) □ **quite unable**: absolutely incapable
flutter and fidget about: move restlessly in all directions □ **her
husband**: Mr Foster □ **must have... state**: certainly knew how she
was feeling □ **privacy**: seclusion □ **cool, dry**: cold, unfriendly
they had..., had they not?: it was time to leave, was it not? (formal
for: "wasn't it?")
a right: an excuse
foolishness: stupidity □ **wife and husband form a couple**
... misery: making her feel more unhappy □ **keeping...**: delaying
her □ **mind you**: note that □ **by no means**: not at all
yet: but □ **whenever**: each time □ **they were** (supposed) **to go**
timing: calculations about time □ **accurate**: exact
manner: behaviour □ **bland**: suave □ **hard**: difficult
believe: be convinced □ **purposely**: intentionally □ **nasty**: unkind
of his own: personal □ **unhappy lady**: miserable woman
dare: venture □ **call out**: shout
tell him: ask him □ **hurry**: be quick, hasten; hurry up!

that. He must also have known that if he was prepared to wait even beyond the last moment of safety, he could drive her nearly into hysterics. On one or two special occasions in the later years of their married life, it seemed almost as though he had *wanted* to miss the train simply in order to intensify the poor woman's suffering.

Assuming (though one cannot be sure) that the husband was guilty, what made his attitude doubly unreasonable was the fact that, with the exception of this one small
10 irrepressible foible, Mrs. Foster was and always had been a good and loving wife. For over thirty years, she had served him loyally and well. There was no doubt about this. Even she, a very modest woman, was aware of it, and although she had for years refused to let herself believe that Mr. Foster would ever consciously torment her, there had been times recently when she had caught herself beginning to wonder.

Mr. Eugene Foster, who was nearly seventy years old, lived with his wife in a large six-storey house in New York
20 City, on East Sixty-second Street, and they had four servants. It was a gloomy place, and few people came to visit them. But on this particular morning in January, the house had come alive and there was a great deal of bustling about. One maid was distributing bundles of dust sheets to every room, while another was draping them over the furniture. The butler was bringing down suitcases and putting them in the hall. The cook kept popping up from the kitchen to have a word with the butler, and Mrs. Foster herself, in an old-fashioned fur coat and with a black hat on the top of
30 her head, was flying from room to room and pretending to supervise these operations. Actually, she was thinking of nothing at all except that she was going to miss her plane

122

know: know, knew, known
beyond: after □ **safety** ≠ risk, danger
(drive) her into hysterics: make her become hysterical
later: just preceding □ **it seemed (as though)**: it gave the impression
that □ **wanted**: decided □ **in order to**: so as to (intention)

assuming: supposing
guilty: not innocent □ **doubly**: twice □ **unreasonable**: not
acceptable
irrepressible foible: uncontrollable defect
loving: affectionate □ **over**: more than

aware: conscious □ **although**: in spite of the fact that
let herself believe: formal for "believe"
ever: cf. never
times: several occasions □ **caught herself... (wonder)**: realized that
she was having her doubts

large: big □ **storey** (Am.): floor or level in a building
East...: the 62nd street (streets have numbers in the US), East Side,
Manhattan □ **gloomy**: unpleasant, dismal □ **few**: not a lot of
January: first month of the year
come alive: livened up □ **...bustling...**: a lot of agitation
maid: female servant □ **bundle(s)**: pile □ **dust sheet(s)**: piece of
material used to protect the **furniture** (tables, chairs...)
butler: head servant □ **suitcase(s)**: case for clothes
the cook prepares meals □ **kept popping up**: frequently appeared
have a word with: say one or two things to
old-fashioned: outdated □ **fur**: animal skin with the hair on
flying: moving quickly; fly, flewn, flown
actually: in reality, in fact

123

if her husband didn't come out of his study soon and get ready.

"What time is it, Walker?" she said to the butler as she passed him.

"It's ten minutes past nine, Madam."

"And has the car come?"

"Yes, Madam, it's waiting. I'm just going to put the luggage in now."

"It takes an hour to get to Idlewild," she said. "My plane
10 leaves at eleven. I have to be there half an hour beforehand for the formalities. I shall be late. I just *know* I'm going to be late."

"I think you have plenty of time, Madam," the butler said kindly. "I warned Mr. Foster that you must leave at nine-fifteen. There's still another five minutes."

"Yes, Walker, I know, I know. But get the luggage in quickly, will you please?"

She began walking up and down the hall, and whenever the butler came by, she asked him the time. This, she kept
20 telling herself, was the *one* plane she must not miss. It had taken months to persuade her husband to allow her to go. If she missed it, he might easily decide that she should cancel the whole thing. And the trouble was that he insisted on coming to the airport to see her off.

"Dear God," she said aloud. "I'm going to miss it. I know, I know, I *know* I'm going to miss it." The little muscle beside the left eye was twitching madly now. The eyes themselves were very close to tears.

"What time is it, Walker?"
30 "It's eighteen minutes past, Madam."

"Now I really *will* miss it!" she cried. "Oh, I wish he would come!"

124

study: personal room for work □ **soon**: before long, shortly

say, **said**, said

Madam: used when addressing a woman (different from: Mrs.)
has the car come?: is the car here yet?
waiting for sth. or sb.
luggage: a traveller's cases, bags, boxes...; baggage (Am.)
it takes...: (time); how long...? □ **Idlewild** = Kennedy Airport
leaves: takes off □ **have to**: must □ **beforehand**: in advance
shall: auxiliary, in the future (inevitability)

plenty of: a lot of, lots of
kindly: nicely □ **warned**: told (in advance) □ **nine-(fifteen)**: (a)
quarter past 9 □ **still... 5 mn**: 5 mn more, 5 mn left
get... in: put... into the car
quickly: rapidly, fast □ **will you please?**: (polite request)
begin, **began**, begun □ **up and down**: backwards and forwards
came by: came near □ **kept** + ing: keep doing sth. = do sth.
repeatedly □ **telling**: saying to □ **the one**: (emphatic)
take, took, **taken** □ **allow**: permit; allow sb. to do sth.
might easily: (strong probability) □ **cancel**: revoke
the whole thing: everything □ **insisted on** + ing
see her off: accompany her and stay until her plane leaves
Dear God: (excl.) My God □ **aloud**: in a loud (≠ quiet) voice

beside: near, next to □ **madly**: with great speed and energy
close to tears: nearly crying or in tears; a teardrop

cried: exclaimed □ **I wish he would**: if only he could (expressing
a strong wish)

This was an important journey for Mrs. Foster. She was going all alone to Paris to visit her daughter, her only child, who was married to a Frenchman. Mrs. Foster didn't care much for the Frenchman, but she was fond of her daughter, and, more than that, she had developed a great yearning to set eyes on her three grandchildren. She knew them only from the many photographs that she had received and that she kept putting up all over the house. They were beautiful, these children. She doted on them, and each time a new
10 picture arrived she would carry it away and sit with it for a long time, staring at it lovingly and searching the small faces for signs of that old satisfying blood likeness that meant so much. And now, lately, she had come more and more to feel that she did not really wish to live out her days in a place where she could not be near these children, and have them visit her, and take them for walks, and buy them presents, and watch them grow. She knew, of course, that it was wrong and in a way disloyal to have thoughts like these while her husband was still alive. She knew also that
20 although he was no longer active in his many enterprises, he would never consent to leave New York and live in Paris. It was a miracle that he had ever agreed to let her fly over there alone for six weeks to visit them. But, oh, how she wished she could live there always, and be close to them!

"Walker, what time is it?"

"Twenty-two minutes past, Madam."

As he spoke, a door opened and Mr. Foster came into the hall. He stood for a moment, looking intently at his wife, and she looked back at him — at this diminutive but still
30 quite dapper old man with the huge bearded face that bore such an astonishing resemblance to those old photographs of Andrew Carnegie.

126

journey: trip; go on a journey = travel
all alone: by herself □ **daughter**: female child
didn't care...: didn't really like
was fond of: really liked, loved
more than that: moreover □ **great yearning**: strong desire
set eyes on: see □ **her grandchildren**: her daughter's children

putting up: displaying □ **all over**: everywhere in
doted on them: loved them madly, was mad about them □ **each**:
every □ **picture**: photo(graph)
staring at: looking fixedly at □ **searching**: scrutinizing
for: to find □ **blood likeness**: family resemblance
meant so much: had so much importance □ **lately**: recently
feel: think □ **wish**: want □ **live out**: spend her whole life

take them for walks: go walking with them □ **buy**: offer
grow (up): develop, become older; grow, grew, grown
wrong: bad □ **in a way**: in some respects □ **thought(s)**: idea
still alive: still living, not dead yet

consent: accept, agree
let: sb. do sth. □ **fly**: travel by plane
six weeks: one and a half month □ **how**: (exclamatory)
always: forever □ **close to**: near, next to

speak, **spoke**, spoken □ **came into**: entered; come, came, come
stand, **stood**, stood □ **intently**: fixedly
diminutive: very small, tiny □ **still**: nevertheless, yet
dapper: neat and active □ **huge**: very big □ **bearded**: *barbu*
...resemblance: looked so much like; bear a resemblance to
A. Carnegie (1835-1919): Am. industrialist and philanthropist

127

"Well," he said. "I suppose perhaps we'd better get going fairly soon if you want to catch that plane."

"*Yes*, dear — *yes!* Everything's ready. The car's waiting."

"That's good," he said. With his head over to one side, he was watching her closely. He had a peculiar way of cocking the head and then moving it in a series of small, rapid jerks. Because of this and because he was clasping his hands up high in front of him, near the chest, he was
10 somehow like a squirrel standing there — a quick clever old squirrel from the Park.

"Here's Walker with your coat, dear. Put it on."

"I'll be with you in a moment," he said. "I'm just going to wash my hands."

She waited for him, and the tall butler stood beside her, holding the coat and the hat.

"Walker, will I miss it?"

"No, Madam," the butler said. "I think you'll make it all right."

20 Then Mr. Foster appeared again, and the butler helped him on with his coat. Mrs. Foster hurried outside and got into the hired Cadillac. Her husband came after her, but he walked down the steps of the house slowly, pausing halfway to observe the sky and to sniff the cold morning air.

"It looks a big foggy," he said as he sat down beside her in the car. "And it's always worse out there at the airport. I shouldn't be surprised if the flight's cancelled already."

"Don't say that, dear — *please*."

They didn't speak again until the car had crossed over the
30 river to Long Island.

"I arranged everything with the servants," Mr. Foster said. "They're all going off today. I gave them half-pay for

128

we'd better: we should □ **get going**: set off
fairly: rather
dear: darling (affectionate term)

over...: leaning or tilted □ **side**: the left or right side
watching: observing □ **closely**: carefully □ **peculiar**: strange
cocking: tilting or turning upwards
jerk(s): quick movement □ **clasping**: joining and holding tight
high ≠ low □ **chest**: top front part of the body
squirrel: small animal with a red fur (it loves nuts!) □ **clever**:
intelligent □ **the Park**: the famous Central Park, in New York

wash (one's) **hands** with water and soap or (euphemistic) go to the
toilet; washroom (Am.) = toilet
holding (in his hand)

make it: arrive on time □ **all right**: without any problem

helped (... coat): helped him put his coat on; help, assist
hurried outside: rushed out of the house
hired: you can hire or rent (Am.) a car for a sum of money
steps: stairs □ **pausing**: stopping □ **halfway**: in the middle
the sky above his head □ **sniff**: draw into his nose □ **cold**: fresh
foggy: not clear; fog = thick mist (condensed water vapour)
worse: comparative of "bad"; ≠ better
flight: to fly; a flight □ **cancelled**: called off

speak: talk □ **again**: any more □ **crossed over**: arrived on the other
side of □ **Long Island**: an island, South East of New York City,
where Kennedy Airport (Idlewild) is situated
off: off duty, on holiday (G.B.) or vacation (U.S.)

six weeks and told Walker I'd send him a telegram when we wanted them back."

"Yes," she said. "He told me."

"I'll move into the club tonight. It'll be a nice change staying at the club."

"Yes, dear. I'll write to you."

"I'll call in at the house occasionally to see that everything's all right and to pick up the mail."

"But don't you really think Walker should stay there all
10 the time to look after things?" she asked meekly.

"Nonsense. It's quite unnecessary. And anyway, I'd have to pay him full wages."

"Oh yes," she said. "Of course."

"What's more, you never know what people get up to when they're left alone in a house," Mr. Foster announced, and with that he took out a cigar and, after snipping off the end with a silver cutter, lit it with a gold lighter.

She sat still in the car with her hands clasped together tight under the rug.

20 "Will you write to me?" she asked.

"I'll see," he said. "But I doubt it. You know I don't hold with letter-writing unless there's something specific to say."

"Yes, dear, I know. So don't you bother."

They drove on, along Queens Boulevard, and as they approached the flat marshland on which Idlewild is built, the fog began to thicken and the car had to slow down.

"Oh dear!" cried Mrs. Foster. "I'm *sure* I'm going to miss it now! What time is it?"

30 "Stop fussing," the old man said. "It doesn't matter anyway. It's bound to be cancelled now. They never fly in this sort of weather. I don't know why you bothered to

130

tell, **told**, told □ **send** a message, a letter, a telegram...

move into: take up residence in □ **tonight**: this evening
staying: living temporarily □ **club**: private house where members
meet (many Americans belong to a club or clubs)
call in: make a short visit □ **occasionally**: now and then
pick up: collect □ **mail** (Am.): letters, etc.; **mailbox** (Am.)

look after: take care of □ **meekly**: humbly
nonsense: that's absurd □ **I'd have to**: I would be obliged to
full wages: a whole salary
of course: I understand
what's more: in addition □ **get up to** sth.: (fam.) do sth. bad

snipping off: cutting off
end: tip □ **silver; gold**: precious metals □ **light, lit**, lit
still: without moving, motionless
rug: piece of thick warm material used as a blanket

I doubt it: I don't think so □ **hold with**: approve of
unless: except when, except if

don't (you) bother: don't take the trouble
drove on: drive, drove, driven ("on" for continuation)
flat ≠ hilly □ **marshland**: *marécage* □ **built**: situated; cf. build
thicken: become thick or dense □ **slow down**: go slower
oh dear!: exclamation expressing anxiety

stop fussing: *arrête ton cinéma!* □ **it doesn't matter**: it doesn't make
any difference □ **bound to**: certain to
... weather: in such weather conditions

come out."

She couldn't be sure, but it seemed to her that there was suddenly a new note in his voice, and she turned to look at him. It was difficult to observe any change in his expression under all that hair. The mouth was what counted. She wished, as she had so often before, that she could see the mouth clearly. The eyes never showed anything except when he was in a rage.

"Of course," he went on, "if by any chance it *does* go,
10 then I agree with you — you'll be certain to miss it now. Why don't you resign yourself to that?"

She turned away and peered through the window at the fog. It seemed to be getting thicker as they went along, and now she could only just make out the edge of the road and the margin of grassland beyond it. She knew that her husband was still looking at her. She glanced at him again, and this time she noticed with a kind of horror that he was staring intently at the little place in the corner of her left eye where she could feel the muscle twitching.

20 "Won't you?" he said.

"Won't I what?"

"Be sure to miss it now if it goes. We can't drive fast in this muck."

He didn't speak to her any more after that. The car crawled on and on. The driver had a yellow lamp directed on to the edge of the road, and this helped him to keep going. Other lights, some white and some yellow, kept coming out of the fog towards them, and there was an especially bright one that followed close behind them all the
30 time.

Suddenly, the driver stopped the car.

"There!" Mr. Foster cried. "We're stuck. I knew it."

it seemed to her : she had the feeling (the impression) that
new note : different tone

hair : (no "s") □ **mouth :** lips (upper and lower lips)
so often : so many times, on so many occasions ; how often?
showed : disclosed
in a rage : in a fury (= intense anger)
went on : added □ **if... it does go :** if it leaves, which I doubt
agree with : share the same opinion as ; ≠ disagree

away : to the other side □ **peered :** looked searchingly
getting thicker : thickening (cf. preceding page, 1. 27)
make out : distinguish □ **edge :** limit
margin : border □ **grassland :** grass is green and grows along the
road □ **still :** expresses continuation □ **glanced :** looked quickly
noticed : noted, saw □ **kind :** sort

feel, felt, felt (a sensation)
won't : will not (future negative)

fast : quickly, at a high speed
muck : (fam.) thick fog, really bad weather ; peasouper (fam.) =
thick yellow fog ; lousy or rotten weather (fam.)
crawled : moved very slowly
keep going : drive on
light(s) : headlight(s) or headlamp(s) at the front of a vehicle
towards them : in their direction
bright : brilliant □ **followed :** came after ; don't look back,
someone's following us!

... stuck : we can't go further □ **I knew it :** I was sure it would happen

133

"No, sir," the driver said, turning round. "We made it. This is the airport."

Without a word, Mrs. Foster jumped out and hurried through the main entrance into the building. There was a mass of people inside, mostly disconsolate passengers standing around the ticket counters. She pushed her way through and spoke to the clerk.

"Yes," he said. "Your flight is temporarily postponed. But please don't go away. We're expecting this weather to
10 clear any moment."

She went back to her husband who was still sitting in the car and told him the news. "But don't you wait, dear," she said. "There's no sense in that."

"I won't," he answered. "So long as the driver can get me back. Can you get me back, driver?"

"I think so," the man said.

"Is the luggage out?"

"Yes, sir."

"Good-bye, dear," Mrs. Foster said, leaning into the car
20 and giving her husband a small kiss on the coarse grey fur of his cheek.

"Good-bye," he answered. "Have a good trip."

The car drove off, and Mrs. Foster was left alone.

The rest of the day was a sort of nightmare for her. She sat for hour after hour on a bench, as close to the airline counter as possible, and every thirty minutes or so she would get up and ask the clerk if the situation had changed. She always received the same reply — that she must continue to wait, because the fog might blow away at any
30 moment. It wasn't until after six in the evening that the loudspeakers finally announced that the flight had been postponed until eleven o'clock the next morning.

made: make, made, made

jumped out: got off (or out of) the car quickly
main: principal □ **entrance** ≠ exit □ **building**: cf. to build
mass: crowd □ **mostly**: mainly □ **disconsolate**: hopelessly sad
counter(s) or desk □ **she pushed...**: she pushed the people in the
crowd to get to the counter □ **clerk**: man at the counter
postponed: delayed; the meeting is postponed until next Monday
expecting (sth. to happen): hoping (that it will happen)
clear: disperse; the plane will take off as soon as it clears

news (always an "s") piece of information
... no sense...: it's pointless (or useless) to wait
so long as or as long as: on condition that, provided
get me back: drive me back home
I think so: "so" is used as a substitute for a whole sentence; will
he come? I think so, or I don't think so, or he said so

kiss: touch given with the lips □ **coarse**: rough □ **fur**: hair
cheek: side of the face below the eye
have a good trip: have a safe journey, Bon Voyage (very formal)
was left: remained; leave, left, left
nightmare: terrifying dream or (here) experience
sit, **sat**, sat □ **bench**: long seat; a park bench □ **airline**: British
Airways is an airline company □ **every... or so**: once in each 30 mn
approximately ("every" expresses recurrence)
reply: answer
blow away: clear; blow, blew, blown; the wind is blowing
not until: not before □ **six in the evening**: 6 p.m.
loudspeaker(s): public address system (it makes sounds louder)
the next (morning): the following morning, the morning after

Mrs. Foster didn't quite know what to do when she heard this news. She stayed sitting on her bench for at least another half-hour, wondering, in a tired, hazy sort of way, where she might go to spend the night. She hated to leave the airport. She didn't wish to see her husband. She was terrified that in one way or another he would eventually manage to prevent her from getting to France. She would have liked to remain just where she was, sitting on the bench the whole night through. That would be the safest. But she
10 was already exhausted, and it didn't take her long to realize that this was a ridiculous thing for an elderly lady to do. So in the end she went to a phone and called the house.

Her husband, who was on the point of leaving for the club, answered it himself. She told him the news, and asked whether the servants were still there.

"They've all gone," he said.

"In that case, dear, I'll just get myself a room somewhere for the night. And don't you bother yourself about it at all."

20 "That would be foolish," he said. "You've got a large house here at your disposal. Use it."

"But, dear, it's *empty*."

"Then I'll stay with you myself."

"There's no food in the house. There's nothing."

"Then eat before you come in. Don't be so stupid, woman. Everything you do, you seem to want to make a fuss about it."

"Yes", she said. "I'm sorry. I'll get myself a sandwich here, and then I'll come on in."

30 Outside, the fog had cleared a little, but it was still a long, slow drive in the taxi, and she didn't arrive back at the house on Sixty-second Street until fairly late.

heard: hear, heard, heard

wondering... way: asking herself, without being able to think clearly □ **spend the night**: sleep for the night □ **hated**: didn't like the idea of (+ ing)
eventually: finally, in the end
manage: succeed in (+ ing) □ **prevent**: stop; prevent sb. from + ing
the whole...: all night □ **the safest**(thing to do): ≠ the most dangerous □ **exhausted**: tired out
elderly: approaching old age □ **lady**: polite term for "woman"
called: (tele)phoned, rang (up)
on the point of (+ ing): about to; he was about to leave

whether: if; I don't know whether they'll come (or not)
gone: left; go, went, gone
somewhere: in a hotel or a motel, for example

foolish: stupid, ridiculous
use it: make use of it, take advantage of it
empty: vacant, unoccupied ≠ full

eat: have your dinner
woman: derogatory term when used to address one's wife! □ **make a fuss**: cf. stop fussing! (3 pages before)
I'm sorry: exlamation expressing apology

drive: journey (by car)

Her husband emerged from his study when he heard her coming in. "Well," he said, standing by the study door, "how was Paris?"

"We leave at eleven in the morning," she answered. "It's definite."

"You mean if the fog clears."

"It's clearing now. There's a wind coming up."

"You look tired," he said. "You must have had an anxious day."

10   "It wasn't very comfortable. I think I'll go straight to bed.

"I've ordered a car for the morning," he said. "Nine o'clock."

"Oh, thank you, dear. And I certainly hope you're not going to bother to come all the way out again to see me off."

"No," he said slowly. "I don't think I will. But there's no reason why you shouldn't drop me at the club on your way."

20   She looked at him, and at that moment he seemed to be standing a long way off from her, beyond some borderline. He was suddenly so small and far away that she couldn't be sure what he was doing, or what he was thinking, or even what he was.

"The club is downtown," she said. "It isn't on the way to the airport."

"But you'll have plenty of time, my dear. Don't you want to drop me at the club?"

"Oh, yes — of course."

30   "That's good. Then I'll see you in the morning at nine."

She went up to her bedroom on the second floor, and she

138

by: near, next to
how was Paris?: what was Paris like?

definite: sure, certain

the **wind** will blow the fog away

straight: immediately, without delay

ordered: asked for; you order a meal at the restaurant; the waiter takes the orders

drop me: set me down □ **on your way**: as you are going to the airport

a long way off: very far away □ **borderline**: limit, frontier

downtown: (in N-Y City) the Lower Side, South of Manhattan; everywhere else in the US "downtown" refers to the town centre

of course: certainly, with pleasure

was so exhausted from her day that she fell asleep soon after she lay down.

Next morning, Mrs. Foster was up early, and by eight-thirty she was downstairs and ready to leave.

Shortly after nine, her husband appeared. "Did you make any coffee?" he asked.

"No, dear. I thought you'd get a nice breakfast at the club. The car is here. It's been waiting. I'm all ready to go."

10 They were standing in the hall — they always seemed to be meeting in the hall nowadays — she with her hat and coat and purse, he in a curiously cut Edwardian jacket with high lapels.

"Your luggage?"

"It's at the airport."

"Ah yes," he said. "Of course. And if you're going to take me to the club first, I suppose we'd better get going fairly soon, hadn't we?"

"Yes!" she cried. "Oh, yes — *please!*"

20 "I'm just going to get a few cigars. I'll be right with you. You get in the car."

She turned and went out to where the chauffeur was standing, and he opened the car door for her as she approached.

"What time is it?" she asked him.

"About nine-fifteen."

Mr. Foster came out five minutes later, and watching him as he walked slowly down the steps, she noticed that his legs were like goat's legs in those narrow stovepipe trousers that 30 he wore. As on the day before, he paused halfway down to sniff the air and to examine the sky. The weather was still not quite clear, but there was a wisp of sun coming through

fell asleep: went to sleep; fall, fell, fallen
lay down: went to bed; lie, lay, lain (in bed, on the grass...)
early ≠ late □ **(eight) thirty:** half past eight
downstairs ≠ upstairs
shortly: a short time, soon

thought: think, thought, thought

meeting: seeing each other □ **nowadays:** these days; ≠ before
purse (Am.): handbag □ **Edwardian... high lapels:** *veste style 1900 à grands revers* (King Edward VII, reigned from 1901 to 1910)

first: before going to the airport

I'll be right with you: I'll be right back, I won't be long

chauffeur: person employed to drive a car for someone else

leg(s): the legs are the 2 lower limbs, the arms the 2 upper limbs
goat: *chèvre* □ **narrow** ≠ wide □ **stovepipe:** *tuyau de poêle*
wore: had on; wear, wore, worn (clothes) □ **as:** like he did

wisp: trace, touch; a wisp of hair, of grass, of smoke...

the mist.

"Perhaps you'll be lucky this time," he said as he settled himself beside her in the car.

"Hurry, please," she said to the chauffeur. "Don't bother about the rug. I'll arrange the rug. Please get going. I'm late."

The man went back to his seat behind the wheel and started the engine.

"*Just* a moment!" Mr. Foster said suddenly. "Hold it a
10 moment, chauffeur, will you?"

"What is it, dear?" She saw him searching the pockets of his overcoat.

"I had a little present I wanted you to take to Ellen," he said. "Now where on earth is it? I'm sure I had it in my hand as I came down."

"I never saw you carrying anything. What sort of present?"

"A little box wrapped up in white paper. I forgot to give it to you yesterday. I don't want to forget it today."

20 "A little box!" Mrs. Foster cried. "I never saw any little box!" She began hunting frantically in the back of the car.

Her husband continued searching through the pockets of his coat. Then he unbuttoned the coat and felt around in his jacket. "Confound it," he said, "I must've left it in my bedroom. I won't be a moment."

"Oh, *please!*" she cried. "We haven't got time! *Please* leave it! You can mail it. It's only one of those silly combs anyway. You're always giving her combs."

30 "And what's wrong with combs, may I ask?" he said, furious that she should have forgotten herself for once.

"Nothing, dear, I'm sure. But..."

mist : thin fog

perhaps : maybe □ **lucky** : successful □ **settled (himself)** : sat down

seat : you sit on it! □ **wheel** or steering-wheel: the driver turns it to change direction □ **engine** : motor

hold it : don't move, stay still (when taking a photo, for example)

overcoat : long warm coat worn over other clothes

on earth : (fam.) emphatic expression used in questions ; what on earth are you doing? ; where on earth have you been?

carrying : holding (in the hand)

box : cardboard container □ **wrapped up** : covered □ **forgot** : didn't remember ; forget, forgot, forgotten

hunting : searching □ **frantically** : excitedly □ **back** ≠ front

unbuttoned : undid the buttons of □ **felt around** : searched with his fingers □ **confound it!** : (fam.) damn it! (expressing strong annoyance) □ **I won't be a moment** : it won't take long

mail (Am.) : post □ **silly** : ridiculous □ **comb(s)** : thing used for arranging hair

may I ask? (he is sarcastically polite)

forgotten herself : lost her self-control □ **for once** : just for this time

"Stay here!" he commanded. "I'm going to get it."

"Be quick, dear! Oh, *please* be quick!"

She sat still, waiting and waiting.

"Chauffeur, what time is it?"

The man had a wristwatch, which he consulted. "I make it nearly nine-thirty."

"Can we get to the airport in an hour?"

"Just about."

At this point, Mrs. Foster suddenly spotted a corner of
10 something white wedged down in the crack of the seat on the side where her husband had been sitting. She reached over and pulled out a small paper-wrapped box, and at the same time, she couldn't help noticing that it was wedged down firm and deep, as though with the help of a pushing hand.

"Here it is!" she cried. "I've found it! Oh dear, and now he'll be up there for ever searching for it! Chauffeur, quickly — run in and call him down, will you please?"

The chauffeur, a man with a small rebellious Irish mouth,
20 didn't care very much for any of this, but he climbed out of the car and went up the steps to the front door of the house. Then he turned and came back. "Door's locked," he announced. "You got a key?"

"Yes — wait a minute." She began hunting madly in her purse. The little face was screwed up tight with anxiety, the lips pushed outward like a spout.

"Here it is! No. I'll go myself. It'll be quicker. I know where he'll be."

She hurried out of the car and up the steps to the front
30 door, holding the key in one hand. She slid the key into the keyhole and was about to turn it — and then she stopped. Her head came up, and she stood here absolutely

144

commanded: ordered; a command, an order

be quick!: hurry up!

wristwatch: watch worn on the wrist (= joint between hand and forearm) □ **I make it...:** what time do you make it?

just about: very nearly, almost

spotted: noticed

wedged: pushed, forced □ **crack:** space between the seats (or the seat and the door) □ **reached (over):** stretched out her hand

pulled out: took out, extracted

couldn't help: couldn't avoid

firm: hard □ **deep:** far down □ **as though... pushing hand:** as if someone had intentionally pushed it with his hand find, **found,** found □ **oh dear:** (excl.) expresses impatience

for ever: for a very long time, for ages

run in: go into the house quickly

Irish: from Ireland

didn't care...: didn't like this very much □ **climbed:** jumped

the front door: the main entrance; ≠ the back door

locked: when the door is locked you need a **key** to unlock it

madly: hurriedly, excitedly, frantically

screwed up tight: very tense

outward: forward □ **spout:** opening from which a liquid comes out (the spout of a teapot, for example)

slid: put; slide, slid, slid

about to: ready to, on the point of (+ ing)

motionless, her whole body arrested right in the middle of all this hurry to turn the key and get into the house, and she waited — five, six, seven, eight, nine, ten seconds, she waited. The way she was standing there, with her head in the air and the body so tense, it seemed as though she were listening for the repetition of some sound that she had heard a moment before from a place far away inside the house.

Yes — quite obviously she was listening. Her whole attitude was a *listening* one. She appeared actually to be moving one of her ears closer and closer to the door. Now it was right up against the door, and for still another few seconds she remained in that position, head up, ear to door, hand on key, about to enter but not entering, trying instead, or so it seemed, to hear and to analyse these sounds that were coming faintly from this place deep within the house.

Then, all at once, she sprang to life again. She withdrew the key from the door and came running back down the steps.

"It's too late!" she cried to the chauffeur. "I can't wait for him, I simply can't. I'll miss the plane. Hurry now, driver, hurry! To the airport!"

The chauffeur, had he been watching her closely, might have noticed that her face had turned absolutely white and that the whole expression had suddenly altered. There was no longer that rather soft and silly look. A peculiar hardness had settled itself upon the features. The little mouth, usually so flabby, was now tight and thin, the eyes were bright, and the voice, when she spoke, carried a new note of authority.

"Hurry, driver, hurry!"

"Isn't your husband travelling with you?" the man

the way...: her attitude
seemed as though: gave the impression that □ **were**: instead of "was" (conditional after "as though") □ **sound**: noise

obviously: evidently
appeared: seemed
ear(s): to hear; an ear
right up against: pressed against

trying: making efforts □ **instead**: in place of that

faintly: not clearly □ **deep within**: far away inside

all at once: suddenly □ **sprang...**: became animated □ **withdrew**: took out

had he been...: if he had (watched her) □ **closely**: carefully
turned: become
altered: changed; an alteration, a change
soft: gentle; ≠ harsh, hard □ **(a peculiar hardness)... features**: his face looked unusually hard
flabby ≠ firm □ **tight**: firmly closed

asked, astonished.

"Certainly not! I was only going to drop him at the club. It won't matter. He'll understand. He'll get a cab. Don't sit there talking, man. *Get going!* I've got a plane to catch for Paris!"

With Mrs. Foster urging him from the back seat, the man drove fast all the way, and she caught her plane with a few minutes to spare. Soon she was high up over the Atlantic, reclining comfortably in her aeroplane chair, listening to the
10 hum of the motors, heading for Paris at last. The new mood was still with her. She felt remarkably strong and, in a queer sort of way, wonderful. She was a trifle breathless with it all, but this was more from pure astonishment at what she had done than anything else, and as the plane flew farther and farther away from New York and East Sixty-second Street, a great sense of calmness began to settle upon her. By the time she reached Paris, she was just as strong and cool and calm as she could wish.

She met her grandchildren, and they were even more
20 beautiful in the flesh than in their photographs. They were like angels, she told herself, so beautiful they were. And every day she took them for walks, and fed them cakes, and bought them presents, and told them charming stories.

Once a week, on Tuesdays, she wrote a letter to her husband — a nice, chatty letter — full of news and gossip, which always ended with the words "Now be sure to take your meals regularly, dear, although this is something I'm afraid you may not be doing when I'm not with you."

When the six weeks were up, everybody was sad that she
30 had to return to America, to her husband. Everybody, that is, except her. Surprisingly, she didn't seem to mind as much as one might have expected, and when she kissed them all

astonished: greatly surprised

It won't matter: there won't be any problem □ **cab**: taxi

urging him: encouraging him

... to spare: a few minutes in advance □ **high up**: far above the ground □ **reclining**: leaning back □ **aeroplane**: or (air)plane
hum: continuous sound □ **heading for**: flying towards □ **mood**: feeling □ **strong**: self-assured □ **queer**: strange
wonderful: very well □ **a trifle**: (fam.) a little □ **breathless**: out-of-breath, short of breath; breathing = respiration
than anything else: than for any other reason
farther: (or further) comparative of "far"

by the time: when □ **reached**: arrived in □ **cool**: serene

met: saw; meet, met, met □ **even**: used to emphasize a comparison
in the flesh: in person, in real life
angels are represented with wings and dressed in white
fed them cakes: gave them cakes (to eat); feed, fed, fed
bought: offered; cf. to buy □ **stories**: Snow White, for example
once: one time □ **on Tuesdays**: every Tuesday □ write, **wrote**, written □ **chatty**: informal and friendly □ **gossip**: details about unimportant matters □ **ended**: finished
meal(s): breakfast, lunch, tea, dinner or supper □ **I'm afraid**: I suspect □ **may**: (possibility)
were up: had passed or elapsed □ **sad**: unhappy

good-bye, there was something in her manner and in the things she said that appeared to hint at the possibility of a return in the not too distant future.

However, like the faithful wife she was, she did not overstay her time. Exactly six weeks after she had arrived, she sent a cable to her husband and caught the plane back to New York.

Arriving at Idlewild, Mrs. Foster was interested to observe that there was no car to meet her. It is possible that
10 she might even have been a little amused. But she was extremely calm and did not overtip the porter who helped her into a taxi with her baggage.

New York was colder than Paris, and there were lumps of dirty snow lying in the gutters of the streets. The taxi drew up before the house on Sixty-second Street, and Mrs. Foster persuaded the driver to carry her two large cases to the top of the steps. Then she paid him off and rang the bell. She waited, but there was no answer. Just to make sure, she rang again, and she could hear it tinkling shrilly far away in the
20 pantry, at the back of the house. But still no one came.

So she took out her own key and opened the door herself.

The first thing she saw as she entered was a great pile of mail lying on the floor where it had fallen after being slipped through the letter box. The place was dark and cold. A dust sheet was still draped over the grandfather clock. In spite of the cold, the atmosphere was peculiarly oppressive, and there was a faint and curious odour in the air that she had never smelled before.
30 She walked quickly across the hall and disappeared for a moment around the corner to the left, at the back. There was something deliberate and purposeful about this action;

manner : attitude, behaviour
hint at : suggest indirectly
in the... future : quite soon
however : but, nevertheless □ **faithful** : loyal
overstay her time : stay longer than she was supposed to
send, **sent**, sent □ **cable** : telegram

overtip : give an exceedingly big tip to; tip = money given for services (to a porter, a waiter, etc.)
lump(s) : small solid mass; a lump of sugar
dirty ≠ immaculate □ **snow** falls from clouds in flakes □ **gutter(s)** : channel along the road for carrying away rainwater
top ≠ bottom
pay, **paid**, paid □ **rang** : you ring **the bell** when you want sb. to come and open the door □ **to make sure** : for confirmation
tinkling : sounding, ringing □ **shrilly** : piercingly
pantry : small room where provisions and cooking utensils are kept
her own key : the key she had for her personal use

great : big
fallen : fall, fell, fallen (on the ground) □ **slipped** : inserted
dark ≠ light
grandfather clock : clock in a tall wooden case that stands on the floor
faint : indistinct, vague □ **odour** : smell
smelled : or smelt (through the nose)

deliberate, purposeful : intentional

151

she had the air of a woman who is off to investigate a rumour or to confirm a suspicion. And when she returned a few seconds later, there was a little glimmer of satisfaction on her face.

She paused in the centre of the hall, as though wondering what to do next. Then, suddenly, she turned and went across into her husband's study. On the desk she found his address book, and after hunting through it for a while she picked up the phone and dialled a number.

10   "Hello," she said. "Listen — this is Nine East Sixty-second Street... Yes, that's right. Could you send someone round as soon as possible, do you think? Yes, it seems to be stuck between the second and third floors. At least, that's where the indicator's pointing... Right away? Oh, that's very kind of you. You see, my legs aren't any too good for walking up a lot of stairs. Thank you so much. Good-bye."

She replaced the receiver and sat there at her husband's desk, patiently waiting for the man who would be coming 20 soon to repair the lift.

air: appearance □ **off**: on her way □ **investigate**: find out information about, make a search or inquiry about

glimmer: small light or sign

wondering: asking herself; I wonder what to do

desk: piece of furniture with a flat top to write on

for a while: for some time

picked up... dialled: when you make a phone call you pick up the receiver, then you dial your number and the telephone rings at the other end of the line □ **(send someone) round**: send a repairman to my house

right away: straight away, immediately

... kind of you: used to express gratitude □ **any too good**: good enough □ **so much**: (emphatic) very much

repair: mend; my T.V. is out of order, I must have it repaired

Grammaire au fil des nouvelles

Traduisez les phrases suivantes inspirées du texte (le premier chiffre renvoie aux pages, les suivants aux lignes) :

Elle le servait fidèlement et bien depuis plus de trente ans (*for* +...?, 122 - 11,12).

Mettez les bagages à l'intérieur, voulez-vous s'il vous plaît ?(demande polie : *will*..., 124 - 16,17).

Oh, je voudrais qu'il vienne ! (expression d'un souhait : *wish* + conditionnel, 124 - 31,32).

Chaque fois qu'une nouvelle photo arrivait elle l'emportait (forme fréquentative avec *would*, 126 - 9,10).

Le brouillard commença à épaissir et la voiture dut ralentir (*to begin* + infinitif ou gérondif ; équivalent de *must*, 130 - 27).

Elle se tourna pour le regarder (infinitif de but, 132 - 3,4).

Sans un mot, Mrs. Foster sauta à l'extérieur et entra précipitamment dans le bâtiment par la porte principale (prépositions et postpositions, 134 - 3,4).

Nous pensons que le temps va s'éclaircir d'un moment à l'autre(*to expect* + proposition infinitive, 134 - 9,10).

Je pense que oui (134 - 16).

Ce serait (ça) le plus prudent (superlatif, 136 - 9).

Tu as dû avoir une journée éprouvante (supposition concernant le passé *must* +...?).

Elle le vit fouiller dans les poches de son pardessus (verbe de perception + gérondif ou infinitif).

Une fois par semaine, *le mardi*, elle écrivait une lettre à son mari (148 - 24,25).

DIP IN THE POOL

Trempé ds les enchères

"Nothing *risqué* ventured, nothing gained", they say. But taking risks does not always pay off, as we shall see in this story.

On the morning of the third day, the sea calmed. Even the most delicate passengers—those who had not been seen around the ship since sailing time—emerged from their cabins and crept on to the sun deck where the deck steward gave them chairs and tucked rugs around their legs and left them lying in rows, their faces upturned to the pale, almost heatless January sun.

It had been moderately rough the first two days, and this sudden calm and the sense of comfort that it brought
10 created a more genial atmosphere over the whole ship. By the time evening came, the passengers, with twelve hours of good weather behind them, were beginning to feel confident, and at eight o'clock that night the main dining-room was filled with people eating and drinking with the assured, complacent air of seasoned sailors.

The meal was not half over when the passengers became aware, by the slight friction between their bodies and the seats of their chairs, that the big ship had actually started rolling again. It was very gentle at first, just a slow, lazy
20 leaning to one side, then to the other, but it was enough to cause a subtle, immediate change of mood over the whole room. A few of the passengers glanced up from their food, hesitating, waiting, almost listening for the next roll, smiling nervously, little secret glimmers of apprehension in their eyes. Some were completely unruffled, some were openly smug, a number of the smug ones making jokes about food and weather in order to torture the few who were beginning to suffer. The movement of the ship then became rapidly more and more violent, and only five or six minutes after
30 the first roll had been noticed, she was swinging heavily from side to side, the passengers bracing themselves in their chairs, leaning against the pull as in a car cornering.

third: 3rd; first, 1st; second, 2nd □ **even**: (intensifier)
the most + adj.: superlative □ **those**: the ones (pl. of "that")
ship: large seagoing vessel □ **sailing time**: departure
crept: walked slowly; cf. to creep □ **sun deck**: outside platform
tucked rugs... legs: *enveloppa leurs jambes dans des couvertures*
lying in rows: reclining side by side □ **almost**: nearly
heatless: which produces no heat; the heat, hot (adj.)
rough: turbulent, stormy; ≠ calm
sense: impression □ **brought**: produced; bring, brought, brought
genial: pleasant, friendly □ **over... ship**: everywhere on board
(by) the time: when

confident: assured □ **main**: principal □ **dining-room**: room where
meals are served □ **filled with**: full of; ≠ empty
complacent: self-satisfied □ **seasoned**: experienced □ **sailors**:
seamen □ **the meal... over**: they had not eaten half their dinner yet
... aware: realized □ **slight**: small □ **bodies**: cf. the human body
seat(s): horizontal part of a chair □ **actually**: really
rolling: swinging from side to side □ **slow** ≠ quick □ **lazy** ≠
vigorous □ **leaning**: cf. the Leaning Tower of Pisa □ **enough**:
sufficient □ **mood**: atmosphere
a few: some □ **glanced up**: looked quickly upwards
listening for: concentrating to hear □ **next**: following
glimmer(s): light, small sign; a glimmer of hope, of interest...
unruffled: calm, unperturbed □ **openly**: visibly, evidently
smug: excessively self-satisfied □ **making jokes**: telling funny
stories □ **in order to**: with the intention of (+ ing)

more and more: increasingly □ **only**: not more than
she: a ship is often personified as "she" □ **heavily**: strongly
bracing themselves: preparing themselves for the shock
pull: horizontal bar □ **... cornering**: when a car turns a corner

At last the really bad roll came, and Mr. William Botibol, sitting at the purser's table, saw his plate of poached turbot with hollandaise sauce sliding suddenly away from under his fork. There was a flutter of excitement, everybody reaching for plates and wineglasses. Mrs. Renshaw, seated at the purser's right, gave a little scream and clutched that gentleman's arm.

"Going to be a dirty night," the purser said, looking at Mrs. Renshaw. "I think it's blowing up for a very dirty
10 night." There was just the faintest suggestion of relish in the way he said it.

A steward came hurrying up and sprinkled water on the tablecloth between the plates. The excitement subsided. Most of the passengers continued with their meal. A small number, including Mrs. Renshaw, got carefully to their feet and threaded their ways with a kind of concealed haste between the tables and through the doorway.

"Well," the purser said, "there she goes." He glanced around with approval at the remainder of his flock who
20 were sitting quiet, looking complacent, their faces reflecting openly that extraordinary pride that travellers seem to take in being recognized as "good sailors."

When the eating was finished and the coffee had been served, Mr. Botibol, who had been unusually grave and thoughtful since the rolling started, suddenly stood up and carried his cup of coffee around to Mrs. Renshaw's vacant place, next to the purser. He seated himself in her chair, then immediately leaned over and began to whisper urgently in the purser's ear. "Excuse me," he said, "but could you tell
30 me something please?"

The purser, small and fat and red, bent forward to listen. "What's the trouble, Mr. Botibol?"

158

at last: finally; ≠ at first

purser: officer who keeps the accounts and takes care of the passengers □ **sliding (away)**: escaping

fork: knife and fork are used at table □ **flutter**: quick movements

reaching for: trying to catch □ **seated**: sitting

right ≠ left (side) □ **scream**: loud cry □ **clutched**: seized

dirty: (fam.) bad, stormy; dirty weather

blowing up for: beginning to develop into

the faintest... relish: a touch of enjoyment

way: manner

hurrying up: walking quickly □ **sprinkled**: poured out (in drops)

tablecloth: cloth covering the table □ **subsided**: diminished

most of: the majority of

carefully: prudently □ **(got) to their feet**: stood up

threaded...: carefully made their way □ **... haste**: hurrying without making it too visible □ **... doorway**: out of the room

approval: approbation □ **remainder**: rest □ **flock**: group of people (also flock of sheep, goats, birds) □ **reflecting**: showing

pride: self-esteem; take pride in, be proud of

recognized: identified

unusually grave: more serious than he usually was

thoughtful: meditative, reflective □ **stood up**: stand, stood, stood

vacant: unoccupied, free; vacancies = free rooms in a hotel

next to: near, by

whisper: speak quietly (in sb.'s ear) □ **urgently**: insistently

tell (me sth.): give me some information

small ≠ tall □ **fat**: corpulent □ **bent forward**: leaned to the front

what's the trouble?: what's the matter?; what's the problem?

"What I want to know is this." The man's face was anxious and the purser was watching it. "What I want to know is will the captain already have made his estimate on the day's run—you know, for the auction pool? I mean before it began to get rough like this?" *agité*

The purser, who had prepared himself to receive a personal confidence, smiled and leaned back in his seat to relax his full belly. "I should say so—yes," he answered. He didn't bother to whisper his reply, although automatically
10 he lowered his voice, as one does when answering a whisperer. *chuchoteur*

"About how long ago do you think he did it?"

"Some time this afternoon. He usually does it in the afternoon."

"About what time?"

"Oh, I don't know. Around four o'clock I should guess."

"Now tell me another thing. How does the captain decide which number it shall be? Does he take a lot of trouble over
20 that?"

The purser looked at the anxious frowning face of Mr. Botibol and he smiled, knowing quite well what the man was driving at. "Well, you see, the captain has a little conference with the navigating officer, and they study the weather and a lot of other things, and then they make their estimate."

Mr. Botibol nodded, pondering this answer for a moment. Then he said, "Do you think the captain knew there was bad weather coming today?"
30 "I couldn't tell you," the purser replied. He was looking into the small black eyes of the other man, seeing the two single little sparks of excitement dancing in their centres. "I

160

already: by now □ **estimate**: calculation
run: distance travelled □ **the auction pool**: *les enchères*
before ≠ after □ **get** + adj.: become; get tired; get angry...

smiled: had a smile on his face, looked amused
belly: stomach □ **I should say so**: I think so
bother: take the trouble □ **reply**: answer □ **although**: though, but
lowered his voice: spoke more quietly □ **one**: anyone
a whisperer: sb. who whispers
about: approximately □ **how long ago**: how many minutes (or hours) before now

around: about □ **I should guess**: I suppose

another thing: something else
... take a lot of trouble...: does he do it very seriously?

frowning: worried; frown = serious look causing lines on the forehead □ **quite well**: very well, perfectly
driving at: suggesting indirectly, hinting at
conference: meeting and discussion □ **study**: examine
weather (conditions); weather forecast = future weather conditions
nodded: moved his head up and down □ **pondering**: meditating upon □ know, **knew**, known

I couldn't tell you: I've got no idea, I don't know

single: only one (in each eye) □ **spark(s)**: light

really couldn't tell you, Mr. Botibol. I wouldn't know."

"If this gets any worse it might be worth buying some of the low numbers. What do you think?" The whispering was more urgent, more anxious now.

"Perhaps it will," the purser said. "I doubt whether the old man allowed for a really rough night. It was pretty calm this afternoon when he made his estimate."

The others at the table had become silent and were trying to hear, watching the purser with that intent, half-cocked,
10 listening look that you can see also at the race track when they are trying to overhear a trainer talking about his chance: the slightly open lips, the upstretched eyebrows, the head forward and cocked a little to one side —that desperately straining, half-hypnotized, listening look that comes to all of them when they are hearing something straight from the horse's mouth.

"Now suppose *you* were allowed to buy a number, which one would *you* choose today?" Mr. Botibol whispered.

"I don't know what the range is yet," the purser patiently
20 answered. "They don't announce the range till the auction starts after dinner. And I'm really not very good at it anyway. I'm only the purser, you know."

At that point Mr. Botibol stood up. "Excuse me, all," he said, and he walked carefully away over the swaying floor between the other tables, and twice he had to catch hold of the back of a chair to steady himself against the ship's roll.

"The sun deck, please," he said to the elevator man.

The wind caught him full in the face as he stepped out
30 on to the open deck. He staggered and grabbed hold of the rail and held on tight with both hands, and he stood there looking out over the darkening sea where the great waves

162

worse ≠ better □ **it might be worth buying... :** it could be profitable to acquire... □ **low** ≠ high ; 1 and 2 are low numbers

perhaps : maybe □ **I doubt whether... :** I don't think...
old man : captain □ **allowed for :** anticipated □ **pretty :** (fam.) rather ; it's pretty cold in here!
trying : attempting ; try to do sth.
watching : observing □ **intent :** fixed □ **half-cocked :** cf. 1. 13
race track or turf : track where horse races are run
overhear : hear □ **a trainer** trains horses for racing
slightly : half (open) □ **lips :** mouth □ **the upstretched eyebrows :** *les sourcils levés* □ **cocked :** leaning, bent ; cock one's ears
desperately straining : extremely tense

straight from the horse's mouth : (fam.) from the person concerned
suppose... allowed to... : if you had the possibility to...
choose : decide to buy ; choose sth., make a choice
the range : the limits (maximum and minimum)
till or until : before ; can you wait till tomorrow?
at : (note the preposition) be good or bad at sth.
anyway : in any case □ **only :** nothing more than

swaying : moving
twice : two times □ **catch hold of :** grab, seize
steady himself : keep his balance

elevator : apparatus for transporting people or goods up and down
catch, caught, caught □ **full :** right □ **stepped out :** walked out
staggered : walked unsteadily □ **rail :** horizontal bar
held on tight : grabbed it firmly □ **both :** his two (hands)
darkening : becoming darker □ **wave(s) :** on the surface of the sea

163

were welling up high and white horses were riding against the wind with plumes of spray behind them as they went.

"Pretty bad out there, wasn't it, sir?" the elevator man said on the way down.

Mr. Botibol was combing his hair back into place with a small red comb. "Do you think we've slackened speed at all on account of the weather?" he asked.

"Oh my word yes, sir. We slackened off considerable since this started. You got to <u>slacken off</u> speed in weather
10 like this or you'll be throwing the passengers all over the ship."

relâcher

Down in the smoking-room people were already gathering for the auction. They were grouping themselves politely around the various tables, the men a little stiff in their dinner jackets, a little pink and overshaved and stiff beside their cool white-armed women. Mr. Botibol took a chair close to the auctioneer's table. He crossed his legs, folded his arms, and settled himself in his seat with the rather desperate air of a man who has made a tremendous
20 decision and refuses to be frightened.

The pool, he was telling himself, would probably be around seven thousand dollars. That was almost exactly what it had been the last two days with the numbers selling for between three and four hundred apiece. Being a British ship they dit it in pounds, but he liked to do his thinking in his own currency. Seven thousand dollars was plenty of money. My goodness, yes! And what he would do he would get them to pay him in hundred-dollar bills and he would take it ashore in the inside pocket of his jacket. No problem
30 there. And right away, yes right away, he would buy a Lincoln convertible. He would pick it up on the way from the ship and drive it home just for the pleasure of seeing

welling up: rising □ **white horses...**: (poetical image or metaphor)
spray: water dispersed in very small drops
out there: on the deck
on the way down: as they were going down to a lower level
combing (back into place): arranging, tidying
slackened speed: reduced speed, slowed down
(at) all: in any way □ **on account of**: because of
my word: exclamation □ **considerable**: instead of "considerably"
(familiar language) □ **you got to**: instead of "you've got to"
throwing... all over the ship: causing the passengers to fall
everywhere on the ship
smoking-room: room for those who wish to smoke
gathering: assembling
stiff: formal, not friendly
dinner jacket(s): formal evening jacket □ **overshaved**: close-shaven
(with a razor) □ **cool**: cold □ **white-armed**: having white arms
close to: near □ **crossed his legs**: put one leg above the other
folded: crossed □ **settled himself**: seated himself comfortably
made: to make (not take!) a decision □ **tremendous**: great,
important □ **frightened**: afraid, anxious
pool: amount of money collected from players at the auction and
offered as a prize to the winner
last: previous □ **selling**: being sold (and bought); sell, sold, sold
apiece: each □ **being**: because it was
pound(s): British monetary unit □ **do his thinking**: think, calculate
his own currency: the type of money used in his country
my goodness: excl. of enthusiasm □ **would...**: (plans for the future)
get them to: ask them to, make them □ **bill(s)** (Am.): banknote
ashore: on land; ≠ on board □ **inside** ≠ outside
right away (Am.): immediately
convertible: car with a folding roof □ **pick it up**: take it
drive, drove, driven (a vehicle)

Ethel's face when she came out the front door and looked at it. Wouldn't that be something, to see Ethel's face when he glided up to the door in a brand-new pale-green Lincoln convertible! Hello, Ethel, honey, he would say, speaking very casual. I just thought I'd get you a little present. I saw it in the window as I went by, so I thought of you and how you were always wanting one. You like it, honey? he would say. You like the colour? And then he would watch her face.

10   The auctioneer was standing up behind his table now. "Ladies and gentlemen!" he shouted. "The captain has estimated the day's run, ending midday tomorrow, at five hundred and fifteen miles. As usual we will take the ten numbers on either side of it to make up the range. That makes it five hundred and five to five hundred and twenty-five. And of course for those who think the true figure will be still farther away, there'll be 'low field' and 'high field' sold separately as well. Now, we'll draw the first numbers out of the hat... here we are... five hundred and twelve?"

20   The room became quiet. The people sat still in their chairs, all eyes watching the auctioneer. There was a certain tension in the air, and as the bids got higher, the tension grew. This wasn't a game or a joke; you could be sure of that by the way one man would look across at another who had raised his bid —smiling perhaps, but only the lips smiling, the eyes bright and absolutely cold.

    Number five hundred and twelve was knocked down for one hundred and ten pounds. The next three or four numbers fetched roughly the same amount.

30   The ship was rolling heavily, and each time she went over, the wooden panelling on the walls creaked as if it were going to split. The passengers held on to the arms of their chairs,

166

front door: main door at the front of the house; ≠ back door

glided up: slowly drove up □ **brand-new:** completely new
honey (Am.): darling
casual: in a relaxed, detached way □ **think, thought,** thought
window: shop-window □ **went by:** passed by
wanting: wishing, having a desire for

"Ladies and Gentlemen!": formal opening of a speech □ **shouted:**
said aloud □ **ending:** finishing □ **midday:** twelve o'clock
mile(s): a nautical mile = 1,853 metres
either: both, each □ **make up:** complete

of course: evidently □ **true:** real □ **figure:** number
farther away: not near those figures □ **"low field" and "high field":**
la série basse et la série haute □ **draw:** take

quiet: silent □ **still:** motionless

bid(s): offer (at an auction)
grew: increased, became bigger □ **game:** sth. that is done for fun

raised: increased
bright: shining □ **cold:** unfriendly
knocked down: *adjugé et vendu*

fetched: came to □ **roughly:** approximately □ **amount:** sum

wooden: made of wood (pine, oak...) □ **panelling:** boards □
creaked: made a harsh squeaking sound □ **split:** crack

167

concentrating upon the auction.

"Low field!" the auctioneer called out. "The next number is low field."

Mr. Botibol sat up very straight and tense. He would wait, he had decided, until the others had finished bidding, then he would jump in and make the last bid. He had figured that there must be at least five hundred dollars in his account at the bank at home, probably nearer six. That was about two hundred pounds —over two hundred. This
10 ticket wouldn't fetch more than that.

"As you all know,"the auctioneer was saying, "low field covers every number *below* the smallest number in the range, in this case every number below five hundred and five. So, if you think this ship is going to cover less than five hundred and five miles in the twenty-four hours ending at noon tomorrow, you better get in and buy this number. So what am I bid?"

It went clear up to one hundred and thirty pounds. Others besides Mr. Botibol seemed to have noticed that the
20 weather was rough. One hundred and forty... fifty... There it stopped. The auctioneer raised his hammer.

"Going at one hundred and fifty..."

"Sixty!" Mr. Botibol called, and every face in the room turned and looked at him.

"Seventy!"

"Eighty!" Mr. Botibol called.

"Ninety!"

"Two hundred!" Mr. Botibol called. He wasn't stopping now —not for anyone.
30 There was a pause.

"Any advance on two hundred pounds?"

Sit still, he told himself. Sit absolutely still and don't look

168

called out: said in a loud voice

sat up: sat upright or **straight** (not bent)

jump in: intervene ☐ **last**: final
figured: calculated ☐ **at least**: a minimum of

over: more than; ≠ under, less than
fetch: sell for

covers: includes ☐ **below**: under

less than ≠ more than

noon: midday ☐ **you better**: instead of "you had better"

clear: all the way, completely
besides: as well as, in addition to

raised: lifted ☐ **hammer**: thing used by the auctioneer to strike the table in order to get attention

he wasn't stopping: he had no intention of stopping
not for anyone: not for anything in the world

told himself: said to himself; tell, told, told

169

up. It's unlucky to look up. Hold your breath. No one's going to bid you up so long as you hold your breath.

"Going for two hundred pounds..." The auctioneer had a pink bald head and there were little beads of sweat sparkling on top of it. "Going..." Mr. Botibol held his breath. "Going... Gone!" The man banged the hammer on the table. Mr. Botibol wrote out a cheque and handed it to the auctioneer's assistant, then he settled back in his chair to wait for the finish. He did not want to go to bed before
10 he knew how much there was in the pool.

They added it up after the last number had seen sold and it came to twenty-one hundred-odd pounds. That was around six thousand dollars. Ninety per cent to go to the winner, ten per cent to seamen's charities. Ninety per cent of six thousand was five thousand four hundred. Well — that was enough. He could buy the Lincoln convertible and there would be something left over, too. With this gratifying thought he went off, happy and excited, to his cabin.

When Mr. Botibol awoke the next morning he lay quite
20 still for several minutes with his eyes shut, listening for the sound of the gale, waiting for the roll of the ship. There was no sound of any gale and the ship was not rolling. He jumped up and peered out of the porthole. The sea —Oh Jesus God!— was smooth as glass, the great ship was moving through it fast, obviously making up for time lost during the night. Mr. Botibol turned away and sat slowly down on the edge of his bunk. A fine electricity of fear was beginning to prickle under the skin of his stomach. He hadn't a hope now. One of the higher numbers was certain
30 to win it after this.

"Oh, my God," he said aloud. "What shall I do?"

What, for example, would Ethel say? It was simply not

170

it's unlucky: it brings bad luck □ **hold your breath**: don't breathe (= take air in) □ **so long as**: as long as, if

bald: with no hair on □ **bead(s)**: drop □ **sweat**: perspiration
sparkling: shining in small flashes
going... gone!: *1 fois, 2 fois, 3 fois, adjugé* □ **banged**: hit write, wrote, written □ **handed**: gave

how much: the amount of money
added it up: counted the money from the bids
odd: (fam.) used with a number, meaning "rather more than"
ninety per cent: 90 % ; a percentage
winner ≠ loser □ **seamen's charities**: organizations that provide help to seamen and their families

left over: remaining (a surplus of money) □ **gratifying**: satisfying

awoke: woke up ; awake, awoke, awoken □ **lie, lay, lain** (in bed)
several: some, a few □ **shut**: closed
gale: very strong wind

peered: looked intently □ **porthole**: small round window
smooth: not rough ; smooth as glass ; smooth as silk (comparisons)
fast: quickly □ **obviously**: evidently □ **making up... lost**: catching up on the time they had wasted
edge: border □ **bunk**: bed (on ship, train) □ **fear**: apprehension
prickle: cause a stinging sensation □ **skin**: it covers the body □ **he hadn't a hope**: he was no longer optimistic

171

possible to tell her that he had spent almost all of their two years' savings on a ticket in the ship's pool. Nor was it possible to keep the matter secret. To do that he would have to tell her to stop drawing cheques. And what about the monthly instalments on the television set and the *Encyclopaedia Britannica?* Already he could see the anger and contempt in the woman's eyes, the blue becoming grey and the eyes themselves narrowing as they always did when there was anger in them.

10 "Oh, my God. What *shall* I do?"

There was no point in pretending that he had the slightest chance now —not unless the goddam ship started to go backwards. They'd have to put her in reverse and go full speed astern and keep right on going if he was to have any chance of winning it now. Well, maybe he should ask the captain to do just that. Offer him ten per cent of the profits. Offer him more if he wanted it. Mr. Botibol started to giggle. Then very suddenly he stopped, his eyes and mouth both opening wide in a kind of shocked surprise. For it was

20 at this moment that the idea came. It hit him hard and quick, and he jumped up from his bed, terribly excited, ran over to the porthole and looked out again. Well, he thought, why not? Why ever not? The sea was calm and he wouldn't have any trouble keeping afloat until they picked him up. He had a vague feeling that someone had done this thing before, but that didn't prevent him from doing it again. The ship would have to stop and lower a boat, and the boat would have to go back maybe half a mile to get him, and then it would have to return to the ship, the whole thing.

30 An hour was about thirty miles. It would knock thirty miles off the day's run. That would do it. "Low field" would be sure to win it then. Just so long as he made certain someone

spent: consumed; spend, spent, spent (money or time)
savings: money put aside for future use □ **nor was it**: and it was not □ **to keep the matter secret**: not to tell her the truth
drawing: making or writing (cheques)
monthly instalment(s): money that has to be paid each month
anger: fury; a person who feels anger is an angry person
contempt: disdain; a contemptuous look
narrowing: getting smaller; to narrow ≠ to widen; narrow ≠ wide (adj.)

there was no point in: it was no good □ **slightest**: smallest
not unless: except if □ **goddam**: (sl.) used with a noun to express annoyance □ **backwards**: in reverse, astern □ **full speed**: at the maximum speed □ **keep... going**: continue without stopping
maybe: perhaps

giggle: laugh in an uncontrolled way
wide: completely, fully □ **kind**: sort
hit: struck □ **hard and quick**: with force and suddenly
ran: hurried; run, ran, run

... afloat: staying at the surface of the water □ **picked him up**: lifted him up □ **feeling**: impression
prevent him from (+ ing): keep him or stop him from (+ ing)
lower a boat: send a boat down into the water

knock (off): deduct; when an article is damaged you can have a certain sum knocked off the price in a shop
made certain: made sure, checked that

saw him falling over; but that would be simple to arrange. And he'd better wear light clothes, something easy to swim in. Sports clothes, that was it. He would dress as though he were going up to play some deck tennis —just a shirt and a pair of shorts and tennis-shoes. And leave his watch behind. What was the time? Nine-fifteen. The sooner the better, then. Do it now and get it over with. Have to do it soon, because the time limit was midday.

Mr. Botibol was both frightened and excited when he
10 stepped out on to the sun deck in his sports clothes. His small body was wide at the hips, tapering upward to extremely narrow sloping shoulders, so that it resembled, in shape at any rate, a bollard. His white skinny legs were covered with black hairs, and he came cautiously out on deck, treading softly in his tennis shoes. Nervously he looked around him. There was only one other person in sight, an elderly woman with very thick ankles and immense buttocks who was leaning over the rail staring at the sea. She was wearing a coat of Persian lamb and the collar was
20 turned up so Mr. Botibol couldn't see her face.

He stood still, examining her carefully from a distance. Yes, he told himself, she would probably do. She would probably give the alarm just as quickly as anyone else. But wait one minute, take your time, William Botibol, take your time. Remember what you told yourself a few minutes ago in the cabin when you were changing? You remember that?

The thought of leaping off a ship into the ocean a thousand miles from the nearest land had made Mr. Botibol
30 —a cautious man at the best of times— unusually advertent. He was by no means satisfied yet that this woman he saw before him was *absolutely certain* to give the alarm

174

over: overboard

wear: put on □ **light** ≠ heavy □ **easy to swim in**: convenient for swimming; swim in the sea □ **dress**: put on clothes □ **as though**: as if

leave his watch behind: not take his watch with him; a watch gives the time □ **the sooner the better** is a set phrase

get it over with: be finished with it, have done with it

hip(s): between the leg and the trunk □ **tapering**: narrowing

sloping: going down □ **shoulder(s)**: between the arm and the trunk

shape: form □ **bollard**: *borne d'amarrage* □ **skinny**: very thin

cautiously: with caution or care; carefully

treading softly: walking carefully

in sight: in view □ **elderly**: rather old □ **thick** ≠ thin □ **ankle(s)**: between the foot and the leg □ **buttocks**: *fesses* □ **staring**: looking fixedly □ **Persian lamb**: *astrakan*

turned up: she had turned up the collar of her coat to keep warm

do: be suitable, be good enough for his purpose

anyone else: any other person

remember: don't forget □ **ago**: before, back (in time)

leaping off: jumping off

the nearest: the next □ **land**: coast

at the best of times: usually, when conditions were favourable

advertent: attentive □ **by no means satisfied yet**: not certain at all up to then

when he made his jump. In his opinion there were two
possible reasons why she might fail him. Firstly, she might
be deaf and blind. It was not very probable, but on the other
hand it *might* be so, and why take a chance? All he had to
do was check it by talking to her for a moment beforehand.
Secondly —and this will demonstrate how suspicious the
mind of a man can become when it is working through self-
preservation and fear— secondly, it had occurred to him
that the woman might herself be the owner of one of the
10 high numbers in the pool and as such would have a sound
financial reason for not wishing to stop the ship. Mr.
Botibol recalled that people had killed their fellows for far
less than six thousand dollars. It was happening every day
in the newspapers. So why take a chance on that either?
Check on it first. Be sure of your facts. Find out about it
by a little polite conversation. Then, provided that the
woman appeared also to be a pleasant, kindly human being,
the thing was a cinch and he could leap overboard with a
light heart.

20   Mr. Botibol advanced casually towards the woman and
took up a position beside her, leaning on the rail. "Hullo,"
he said pleasantly.

She turned and smiled at him, a surprisingly lovely,
almost a beautiful smile, although the face itself was very
plain. "Hullo," she answered him.

Check, Mr. Botibol told himself, on the first question.
She is neither blind nor deaf. "Tell me," he said, coming
straight to the point, "what did you think of the auction last
night?"

30   "Auction?" she asked, frowning. "Auction? What
auction?"

"You know, that silly old thing they have in the lounge

176

might: (possibility) □ **fail him**: not do what he wanted her to do
deaf and blind: a deaf person can't hear, a blind one can't see
... hand: used to introduce an opposite point □ **chance**: risk
check: verify, find out about □ **beforehand**: before, in advance

the mind is what enables a person to think □ **working**: functioning
□ **self-preservation**: survival instinct □ **... occurred...**: the idea had
come to his mind □ **be the owner of**: possess
as such: for that reason □ **sound**: good (reason)

recalled: remembered □ **killed**: caused the death of □ **fellow(s)**:
companion; fellow travellers; schoolfellows...
the newspapers: the press

provided that: if, on condition that
appeared: seemed □ **kindly**: friendly, considerate
... a cinch: (sl.) it was sure to succeed (≠ fail)
(with a) light heart: feeling light-hearted (= unworried)

pleasantly: nicely, in a friendly way

plain: ordinary, simple

neither... nor...: not... and not... either
last night: yesterday evening

frowning: with a puzzled look on her face (cf. also p. 161, l. 21)

silly old thing: (fam.) stupid thing □ **lounge**: sitting-room

177

after dinner, selling numbers on the ship's daily run. I just wondered what you thought about it."

She shook her head, and again she smiled, a sweet and pleasant smile that had in it perhaps the trace of an apology. "I'm very lazy," she said. "I always go to bed early. I have my dinner in bed. It's so restful to have dinner in bed."

Mr. Botibol smiled back at her and began to edge away. "Got to go and get my exercise now," he said. "Never miss my exercise in the morning. It was nice seeing you. Very nice
10 seeing you..." He retreated about ten paces, and the woman let him go without looking around.

Everything was now in order. The sea was calm, he was lightly dressed for swimming, there were almost certainly no man-eating sharks in this part of the Atlantic, and there was this pleasant kindly old woman to give the alarm. It was a question now only of whether the ship would be delayed long enough to swing the balance in his favour. Almost certainly it would. In any event, he could do a little to help in that direction himself. He could make a few difficulties
20 about getting hauled up into the lifeboat. Swim around a bit, back away from them surreptitiously as they tried to come up close to fish him out. Every minute, every second gained would help him win. He began to move forward again to the rail, but now a new fear assailed him. Would he get caught in the propeller? He had heard about that happening to persons falling off the sides of big ships. But then, he wasn't going to fall, he was going to jump, and that was a very different thing. Provided he jumped out far enough he would be sure to clear the propeller.

éclaircir

30 Mr. Botibol advanced slowly to a position at the rail about twenty yards away from the woman. She wasn't looking at him now. So much the better. He didn't want her

178

wondered : wanted to know

shook : moved (her head) from left to right □ **sweet :** gentle, kind

apology : expression of regret ; apologize for sth., ask to be excused

early ≠ late

restful : relaxing ; a good night's rest

edge away : walk slowly away

got to go : (fam.) I must go □ physical **exercise** □ **never miss :** I always take □ **... seeing you** (or meeting you) : formal expression of farewell □ **retreated :** walked back □ **pace(s) :** distance covered by a step □ **let him... :** didn't look at him when he left

shark(s) : large grey fish with sharp teeth that can be dangerous to people

whether : if □ **delayed :** made late

in any event : in any case, whatever happened

hauled up : lifted up □ **lifeboat :** special boat used to rescue people in danger at sea □ **a bit :** a little □ **surreptitiously ≠** openly

close : near him □ **fish him out** of the water

propeller : device for producing movement in a ship (or aircraft)

clear : stay clear of, avoid

yard(s) : measure of length (1 yard = 91.44 cm)

so much the better : that was fine

watching him as he jumped off. So long as no one was watching he would be able to say afterwards that he had slipped and fallen by accident. He peered over the side of the ship. It was a long, long drop. Come to think of it now, he might easily hurt himself badly if he hit the water flat. Wasn't there someone who once split his stomach open that way, doing a belly flop from the high dive? He must jump straight and land feet first. Go in like a knife. Yes, sir. The water seemed cold and deep and grey and it made him
10 shiver to look at it. But it was now or never. Be a man, William Botibol, be a man. All right then... now... here goes...

He climbed up on to the wide wooden top-rail, stood there poised, balancing for three terrifying seconds, then he leaped —he leaped up and out as far as he could go and at the same time he shouted "*Help!*"

"*Help! Help!*" he shouted as he fell. Then he hit the water and went under.

When the first shout for help sounded, the woman who
20 was leaning on the rail started up and gave a little jump of surprise. She looked around quickly and saw sailing past her through the air this small man dressed in white shorts and tennis-shoes, spreadeagled and shouting as he went. For a moment she looked as though she weren't quite sure what she ought to do: throw a lifebelt, run away and give the alarm, or simply turn and yell. She drew back a pace from the rail and swung half around facing up to the bridge, and for this brief moment she remained motionless, tense, undecided. Then almost at once she seemed to relax, and
30 she leaned forward far over the rail, staring at the water where it was turbulent in the ship's wake. Soon a tiny round black head appeared in the foam, an arm was raised above

he would be able to : it would be possible for him to

drop : distance (to fall) □ **come to think of it :** on reflection
hurt himself badly : be seriously injured □ **hit the water flat :** came into contact with the sea horizontally
belly flop : *plat-ventre* □ **high dive :** *plongeon de haut vol*
land : hit the water □ **a knife** is used for cutting □ **yes, sir** (Am.) : that's it □ **deep :** going far down from the surface ; ≠ shallow
shiver : tremble, skake (with fear, with cold)
here goes : here we go, let's go

climbed up : went up ; climb up stairs, a tree, a ladder...
poised : balanced, hanging
far : far away ; ≠ near
help! : interjection used to ask for assistance

started up : made a quick movement (of surprise)
sailing (in the air) : flying, moving fast

spreadeagled : with his arms and legs spread out (origin of the word : like an eagle with its wings outstretched)
ought to : should □ **throw** (into the sea) □ **lifebelt :** inflatable belt used to keep a person afloat □ **yell :** shout out loud
swung : turned □ **facing up to :** turned towards □ **bridge :** platform where the captain stands

wake : track left by the ship in water □ **tiny :** very small
foam : white mass of small bubbles on the surface of the sea

181

it, once, twice, vigorously waving, and a small faraway voice
was heard calling something that was difficult to understand. The woman leaned still farther over the rail, trying to
keep the little bobbing black speck in sight, but soon, so
very soon, it was such a long way away that she couldn't
even be sure it was there at all.

After a while another woman came out on deck. This one
was bony and angular, and she wore horn-rimmed
spectacles. She spotted the first woman and walked over to
10 her, treading the deck in the deliberate, military fashion of
all spinsters.

"So *there* you are," she said.

The woman with the fat ankles turned and looked at her,
but said nothing.

"I've been searching for you," the bony one continued.
"Searching all over."

"It's very odd," the woman with the fat ankles said. "A
man dived overboard just now, with his clothes on."

"Nonsense!"

20   "Oh yes. He said he wanted to get some exercise and he
dived in and didn't even bother to take his clothes off."

"You better come down now," the bony woman said. Her
mouth had suddenly become firm, her whole face sharp and
alert, and she spoke less kindly than before. "And don't you
ever go wandering about on deck alone like this again. You
know quite well you're meant to wait for me."

"Yes, Maggie," the woman with the fat ankles answered,
and again she smiled, a tender, trusting smile, and she took
the hand of the other one and allowed herself to be led away
30 across the deck.

"Such a nice man," she said. "He waved to me."

182

waving : moving (as a signal) □ **faraway** : distant

hear, **heard**, heard □ **understand** : perceive

farther or further : (here) more

bobbing : moving up and down quickly □ **speck** : small mark or spot □ **a long way away** : at a long distance

a while : some time

bony : very thin (so that the bones can be seen) □ **horn-rimmed** : *à monture d'écaille* □ **spectacles** : glasses □ **spotted** : saw, recognized

fashion : way, manner

spinster(s) : unmarried woman (who is no longer young)

searching for : looking for, trying to find

all over : everywhere

odd : curious, strange

dived : plunged

nonsense! : (fam.) rubbish!, that's absurd

take (clothes) **off** : undress

sharp : severe ; speak sharply

speak, **spoke**, spoken

wandering : walking about with no aim □ **alone** : unaccompanied

meant to : supposed to ; mean, meant, meant

trusting : confident ; trust sb., rely on sb. □ take, **took**, taken

allowed herself to : let herself □ **led** : guided ; lead, led, led

such a... : : (exclamation) such a nice man, such a beautiful day

183

Grammaire au fil des nouvelles

Traduisez les phrases suivantes inspirées du texte (le premier chiffre renvoie aux pages, les suivants aux lignes) :

Les deux premiers jours (ordre des mots, 156 - 8). **Les trois ou quatre numéros suivants** (166 - 28,29).

Quelques-uns des passagers levèrent les yeux de leur nourriture (quantité indéterminée, 156 - 22). **Certains étaient complètement imperturbables** (156 - 25).

Le mouvement du bateau devint alors rapidement *de plus en plus violent* (156 - 28,29).

La plupart **des passagers continuèrent leur repas** (158 - 14).

Excusez-moi, dit-il, mais pourriez-vous me dire quelque chose s'il vous plaît ? (conditionnel de *can*, composés de *some*, *any*, *no*, 158 - 29,30).

Ils étaient en train de se regrouper poliment autour des différentes tables (pronoms réfléchis, 164 - 13,14).

Que vais-je faire ? (auxiliaire *shall*, 170 - 31).

Il resta allongé complètement immobile *pendant plusieurs* **minutes** *les* **yeux fermés** (170 - 19,20).

Il *ferait mieux de* **porter des vêtements légers** (174 - 1,2).

Le plus tôt (serait) **le mieux** (comparatifs, 174 - 6).

Souviens-toi de *ce que* **tu t'es dit** *il y a quelques* **minutes** (174 - 25).

Premièrement, elle pourrait être sourde et aveugle (auxiliaire exprimant l'éventualité ?, 176 - 2,3).

Elle n'est *ni* **aveugle** *ni* **sourde** (176 - 27).

Un si gentil monsieur ! (exclamation avec *such*, 182 - 31).

Vocabulaire

Voici environ 1 400 mots rencontrés dans les nouvelles, suivis du sens qu'ils ont dans celles-ci.

— A —

able to (be) être capable de

about environ

about to (be) être sur le point de

above; above all au-dessus de ; par-dessus tout

account (bank) compte en banque

account of (on) à cause de

accurate précis

ache faire mal

ache to + verb mourir d'envie de

across à travers

actually en fait, véritablement

ad, advertisement annonce publicitaire

add up additionner

advertent attentif

aerial antenne

afford sth. *(pouvoir)* se permettre qqch.

afloat (keep) flotter

afternoon après-midi

aftertaste arrière-goût

again de nouveau

against contre

ago il y a *(temps)*

agree être d'accord

ahead devant, en avant

aircraft (invariable) avion

airline compagnie d'aviation

airman aviateur

alive vivant

all tous

all over partout *(surface)*

all right d'accord

all the way tout du long

all; at all tout ; du tout

allow permettre, autoriser

almost presque

alone seul

alongside à côté de

aloud à voix haute

already déjà

alter changer

although bien que

altogether tout à fait

always toujours

amazing stupéfiant

amount quantité, somme

anger colère

ankle cheville

annoy agacer, contrarier

answer répondre

anyway de toute façon

apart à part, séparé

apiece chaque

apology excuse

appear apparaître ; sembler

apple pomme

arch malicieux

area région

arm bras

around autour de, environ, aux alentours

as if comme si

as soon as dès que

as such en tant que tel

as though comme si

as well aussi

ashamed of (be) avoir honte de

ashore à terre

asleep endormi

assume supposer

astern (go) reculer

astonishing étonnant

astonishment étonnement

at first d'abord

at once immédiatement

at the most au maximum

auction enchères

auctioneer commissaire-priseur

awake, awoke, awoken se réveiller

aware of (be) être conscient de

awoke (cf. awake)

— B —

back arrière

background arrière-plan

backwards en arrière

bad mauvais

bald chauve

bang frapper violemment

bank bord, rive

bank virer sur l'aile *(aviation)*

bargain (into the) par-dessus le marché

bark aboyer

bashful timide

basket panier

bastard (sl.) salaud

bat manier la batte *(cricket, base-ball)*

bead perle

bear, bore, borne porter

beard; bearded barbe ; barbu

bearing allure

beautiful magnifique

because of à cause de

become, became, become devenir

beer bière

before avant

beforehand à l'avance

187

begin, began, begun commencer

beginning début

behind derrière

being (human) être humain

believe croire

bell sonnette

belly ventre, bedaine

belong to appartenir à

below au-dessous de

belt ceinture

bench banc

bend, bent, bent courber, plier, se pencher

benevolent plein de bonté

beside à côté de

besides en dehors de

best (the) le meilleur

bet; bet (a) parier; pari

betray trahir

better; I'd better meilleur; je ferais mieux de

between entre

bewildered perplexe

beyond au-delà de, plus loin

bid offre *(enchère)*

bike, motorbike moto

bill (Am.) billet de banque

billow out se gonfler

bird oiseau

bit of stuff (sl.) machin, truc

bit; a bit morceau; un peu

black out avoir un étourdissement

blade lame

bland affable

blank vide

blew (cf. blow)

blind aveugle

blithely gaiement

blood sang

bloody (sl.) satané, fichu

blow, blew, blown souffler

boat bateau

bob danser *(sur l'eau)*

body corps; carosserie

bonfire feu de joie

bony maigre

borderline frontière

bored; boredom ennuyé; ennui

born né

both les deux

bother se soucier, se donner la peine

bottom fond

bought (cf. buy)

box boîte

brace oneself se tenir

brain cerveau

brand-new flambant neuf

brass cuivre, laiton

bread pain

break off (broke, broken) interrompre

break out (broke, broken) éclater

break, broke, broken casser

breakfast petit déjeuner

breast poitrine

breath respiration

breathe respirer

breathless (be) avoir le souffle coupé

breeches culotte *(pantalon)*

breed espèce, cru *(vin)*

bricklayer maçon

bridge pont ; passerelle de commandement

bright ; brightness brillant ; éclat

bring, brought, brought apporter

brittle cassant

broke (cf. break)

brought (cf. bring)

brush brosser

bubble bulle

build, built, built construire

building bâtiment

bundle paquet

bunk couchette

burn, burnt, burnt or burned brûler

business truc, affaire

bustle s'agiter, s'affairer

butler majordome

buttock fesse

buy it (fam.) y passer, mourir

buy, bought, bought acheter

by no means aucunement, pas du tout

by the way au fait

— C —

cab taxi

call appeler, téléphoner

call out annoncer

came (cf. come)

cancel annuler

candle bougie

cap casquette

car cornering virage

card-sharper tricheur *(aux cartes)*

card ; card game carte ; jeu de cartes

care, I don't care se soucier de, je m'en fiche

careful (be) faire attention

carefully avec soin, délicatement

carry; carry away porter ; emporter

carve découper *(viande)*

casual décontracté

catch on (caught, caught) piger

catch, caught, caught attraper ; prendre *(train, etc.)*

cautious; cautiously prudent ; prudemment

century siècle

challenge défi

chance; take a chance hasard ; prendre un risque

character personnage

charity œuvre de bienfaisance

charred carbonisé

chat brève conversation

chatty letter lettre pleine de bavardages

cheap bon marché

check, check up vérifier

cheek joue

cheerful gai, jovial

chest poitrine

chew mâcher

child (pl. children) enfant

chin menton

chock cale

choice choix

choose, chose, chosen choisir

cinch (it's a) (sl.) c'est du tout cuit

claret Bordeaux *(vin)*

clasp one's hands joindre les mains

clear s'éclaircir, se dissiper

clearly clairement

clerk employé

clever intelligent

cliff falaise

climb grimper

cling to, clang to, clung to s'accrocher à

clink (sl.) taule *(prison)*

clock horloge, pendule

clockwork mouvement mécanique

close in se rapprocher

close; closely près ; de près

cloth étoffe, toile

clothes (pl.) vêtements

cloud nuage

clutch agripper

coarse grossier ; rugueux

coat manteau

cock dresser

coin pièce de monnaie

collar col

collect ramasser

comb peigne

come off (came, come) se détacher de

come out (came, come) sortir

come round (came, come) faire le tour de

come, came, come venir

comfort bien-être

complacent suffisant

conceal dissimuler

conference entretien

confident assuré

confound it! (fam.) la barbe !

conjurer prestidigitateur

conjuring trick tour de magie

contempt(uous) mépris-s(ant)

contents (pl.) contenu

convertible car voiture décapotable

cook cuisinier

cool; coolness (the) calme, froid ; le calme

copper (sl.) flic

cork bouchon de liège

corner coin

corpse cadavre

cost, cost, cost coûter

count compter

country campagne, pays

couple of (a) deux ou trois

course plat *(partie d'un menu)*

course (of) bien sûr

court tribunal

cover couvrir, parcourir

cow vache

coward lâche

crack espace, fente

crafty malin, rusé

crammed bourré, bondé

crawl avancer lentement

creak craquer

creep, crept, crept ramper, s'approcher discrètement

crisp croquant

cross traverser ; croiser *(jambes)*

crummy (sl.) sale, miteux, minable

currency monnaie

curtain rideau

cut, cut, cut couper

— D —

daddy papa

daft stupide, idiot

daily journalier

damage abîmer

dangle pendre

dapper pimpant, fringant

dare, I dare not oser, je n'ose pas

dark sombre, foncé

darken s'assombrir

darn (sl.) (adv.) vachement

dash se précipiter

daughter fille

dazzle aveugler

dead (adj.) mort

deaf sourd

deal, dealt, dealt distribuer *(les cartes)*

deal (a great) beaucoup

deal with (dealt, dealt) s'occuper de

dear cher

dear! (oh) mon dieu !

death (the) la mort

decent convenable

deck pont *(bateau)*

deep(ness) profond(eur)

definite sûr et certain

delightful délicieux

demure modeste

design motif

desk bureau *(meuble)*

despise mépriser

devil démon

dial a number composer un numéro

diary agenda

die mourir

diffident qui manque d'assurance

dinner jacket smoking

dip tremper

dirty sale

disappear disparaître

disapproval désapprobation

disconsolate inconsolable

dish plat

display montrer

disposal disposition

disturb déranger

dive plonger

do up a button boutonner

do, did, done faire

dot point

dote on être fou de

downstairs en bas

downwards vers le bas

drain away s'écouler

draught courant d'air

draw, drew, drawn tirer, retirer

draw in (drew, drawn) aspirer

drawl parler d'une voix traînante

dreaded redouté, craint

dream rêve

dress s'habiller

drink, drank, drunk boire

drive at (drove, driven) insinuer

drive, drove, driven conduire

driving-licence permis de conduire

droll bizarre

drop laisser tomber; déposer

drove (cf. drive)

dry sec

dual carriageway route à quatre voies

duck soup (sl.) une proie facile

dust poussière

Dutch hollandais

— E —

each; each other chaque; l'un l'autre

eagerly avec empressement

eagerness avidité, impatience

ear oreille

early tôt

earth terre

easy meat (sl.) simple comme bonjour

eat, ate, eaten manger

edge bord, rebord

edge away s'éloigner furtivement

either non plus

elderly assez âgé

elevator (Am.) ascenseur

else, what else autre, quoi d'autre

empty vide

end bout, extrémité

engine moteur

engrossed in absorbé par

enjoy apprécier

enlist s'engager

enough assez

entrance entrée

erect droit

escape s'échapper

even plat, régulier

even (not) même *(pas)*

evening soir

every; everyone; everything chaque; tout le monde; tout

evil mauvais

exciting fascinant

exhausted exténué

expect supposer, s'attendre à

expensive cher

extra supplémentaire

eye œil

eyebrow sourcil

fail décevoir

faint faible

faintly faiblement

fairly assez, plutôt

faithful fidèle

fall, fell, fallen tomber

fancy de luxe

far, by far loin, de loin

faraway distant

farther plus loin

fashion manière

fast rapide, rapidement

fasten fermer *(bouton)*, attacher

fat gros, gras

fatherly paternel

fear crainte, peur

feature trait

feed, fed, fed nourrir

feel for (felt, felt) chercher en tâtant

feel, felt, felt se sentir, ressentir

feeling sensation, impression

feet (cf. foot)

fell (cf. fall)

fellow camarade

fellow (fam.) type

felt (cf. feel)

fetch aller chercher

few (a) quelques

fidget gigoter

fight, fought, fought se battre

fighter, fighter pilot avion de chasse, pilote de chasse

figure calculer

figure (a) chiffre, nombre ; silhouette

file ; filing cabinet dossier ; armoire à dossiers

fill, fill up, fill in remplir

find, found, found ; find out trouver ; découvrir

fine (a) amende, contravention

fine (adj.) bien, beau, excellent ; mince

finger doigt

fire tirer

fire (on) en feu

first ; at first premier ; d'abord

fish plonger la main (dans une poche)

fish (pl. fish or fishes) poisson

fish out repêcher

flabbergasted époustouflé

flabby mou

flap coup

flare s'enflammer

flash éclair

flat plat

flat out à toute allure, à vitesse maximum

flavour saveur

flesh, in the flesh chair, en chair et en os

flew (cf. fly)

flight vol

flip donner un petit coup à

flock troupeau

flog (sl.) fourguer

floor plancher ; étage

flutter s'agiter, voltiger

fly, flew, flown voler, piloter un avion

foam écume

fog; foggy brouillard ; brumeux

foible manie, défaut

fold up plier

follow suivre

fond of (be) aimer

fool imbécile

foolish; foolishness idiot ; stupidité

foot (pl. feet) pied, un pied *(mesure)* = 30,48 cm

footbrake frein à pied

foothold prise *(de pied)*

footstep pas

for ever pour toujours

forget, forgot, forgotten oublier

fork fourche, fourchette

forward en avant

fought (cf. fight)

found (cf. find)

frailty faiblesse

frantically frénétiquement

fried (cf. fry)

frightened of (be) avoir peur de

front, in front of avant, devant

frosty glacé

frown froncer les sourcils

fry frire

full complet

full of plein de, rempli de

fumes (pl.) émanations

fun amusement, plaisir

funny amusant

fur fourrure

further plus loin

fuss, make a fuss faire des histoires

— G —

gale coup de vent

game jeu, partie

gasp haleter

195

gate barrière

gather se rassembler ; déduire *(idée)*

gave (cf. give)

genial chaleureux, cordial

gently doucement

genuine véritable, authentique

German, Germany Allemand, Allemagne

get away from (got, got) s'éloigner de

get back (got, got) retourner, rentrer

get in (got, got) monter *(véhicule)*

get off (got, got) descendre *(véhicule)*

get up (got, got) se lever

get, got, got avoir, recevoir...

get, got, got + adj. devenir

giggle ricaner

girl-friend petite amie, fiancée

give back rendre

give up (gave, given) abandonner

give, gave, given donner

glad heureux

glance at jeter un coup d'œil à

glass verre

glide arriver sans bruit

glimmer briller *(faiblement)*

gloomy morne

glove gant

go back revenir

go by passer

go on + ing (went, gone) continuer à

go on! allez-y !

go past (went, gone) dépasser

go through (went, gone) traverser

go, went, gone aller, s'en aller, partir

gob (sl.) crachat, mollard

God! Mon Dieu !

goddam (sl.) satané

goggles lunettes de protection

gold; goldsmith or ; orfèvre

good and proper bel et bien

good grief! ciel !, grands dieux !

Goodness ! Mon Dieu !

goods marchandises, articles

gossip (invariable) commérages

got (cf. get)

grandchildren petits-enfants

grape raisin

grasp saisir

grass herbe

gratifying agréable

great; greatly formidable ; énormément

grew (cf. grow)

grey; greyish gris ; grisonnant

grin faire un large sourire ou un rictus

ground sol

grow into se transformer en

grow, grew, grown croître, grandir

growl; growling gronder ; grondement

grunt grogner

guess, I guess deviner, je suppose

guest invité

guilty coupable

gun canon

gust of wind rafale de vent

gutter égout

— H —

haircream brillantine, crème capillaire

half, half an hour demi, demi-heure

halfway à mi-chemin

hammer marteau, maillet

hand tendre

hand (on the other) d'autre part

handkerchief mouchoir

handle poignée

hang, hung, hung pendre, être suspendu

happen arriver, se passer

harbour port

hard (adj.); hard (adv.) difficile ; fort, dur

hardly à peine

hardness dureté

harm faire du mal, endommager

haste précipitation

hate détester

haul up hisser

hay (make) faire les foins

hazy embrumé

head tête

head for se diriger vers

head-on de front

hear, heard, heard entendre

heart cœur

heat, heatless chaleur, sans chaleur

heaven ciel

heavily lourdement

hedge haie

hefty lourde, grosse *(somme d'argent)*

height hauteur

held (cf. hold)

helmet casque

help aide, secours

help (I can't) je ne peux pas m'empêcher de

help oneself se servir

helpful utile

helpless impuissant, désarmé

hide, hid, hidden cacher

high haut

hill colline

hint suggérer

hip hanche

hired loué

hit, hit, hit frapper, heurter

hitch up remonter

hitch-hiker auto-stoppeur

hod oiseau, hotte *(terme technique)*

hold it! attendez !

hold out (held, held) tendre

hold, held, held tenir, maintenir

hole trou

home-made fait maison

honey chéri (sens premier : *miel*)

hood capot

hope espérer

horn corne, écaille

horse cheval

host hôte

hour (an) heure

how long ago? il y a combien de temps ?

how much? combien ?

how often? tous les combien de temps ?

however cependant

huffily (fam.) d'un air fâché

huge énorme

hum bourdonnement

hundred (one or a) cent

hunt fouiller

hurry, be in a hurry se précipiter, être pressé

hurt, hurt, hurt faire mal, blesser

— I —

imperious autoritaire

impinge upon empiéter sur

inch (an) un pouce = 2, 54 cm

increase augmenter

incredible incroyable

indeed certes

inflict infliger

inside intérieur, à l'intérieur

instalment remboursement

instance (for) par exemple

instead au lieu de, à la place

intent(ly) fixe(ment)

Irish Irlandais

issue problème

item article

— J —

jab coup (de fourchette)

jacket veste

jam écraser, presser

jaw mâchoire

jeweller bijoutier

job métier, travail

joke; joke (a) plaisanter; plaisanterie

journey voyage

jump; jump in! sauter; montez! *(véhicule)*

— K —

keep steady (kept, kept) maintenir, stabiliser

keep, kept, kept garder

keep, kept, kept + adj. rester

keep, kept, kept + ing continuer à, ne pas cesser de

key; key ring clef; porteclefs

keyhole trou de serrure

kick donner un coup de pied

kid gosse, gamin

kill tuer

kind (a) sorte

kind; kindly gentil; gentiment

king roi

kiss baiser

kitchen cuisine

knee genou

knew (cf. know)

knife (pl. knives) couteau

knob bouton, protubérance

knock off déduire

knock over renverser

knocked down adjugé *(enchère)*

know, knew, known connaître, savoir

knowledge (invariable) connaissances

— L —

lack manquer

ladder échelle

lady (pl. ladies) dame

laid (cf. lay)

lamb; Persian lamb mouton ; astrakan

lamely maladroitement

land; land (the) atterrir ; terre

lane file, voie

lap (invariable) genoux

lapel revers *(vêtement)*

last durer

last (adj.) dernier

late tard, en retard

lately récemment

law, break the law loi, enfreindre la loi

lay (cf. lie)

lay, laid, laid mettre *(la table)*

lazy paresseux, peu énergique

leaf feuille

lean incliner, *(se)* pencher

leap, leapt, leapt (or leaped) bondir

learn, learnt, learnt or learned apprendre

least (at) au moins

leather cuir

leave, left, left quitter, partir

left gauche

left over qui reste

leg jambe

less; none the less moins ; néanmoins

let, let, let laisser

level niveau

lie, lay, lain être étendu, être posé *(objet)*

lie, liar mentir, menteur

life (pl. lives) vie

life-size grandeur nature

lifebelt bouée de sauvetage

lifeboat bateau de sauvetage

lift lever

lift (a) ascenseur

lift (fam.) piquer, faucher

lift (give sb. a) prendre qqn dans sa voiture

light lumière

light, lit, lit or lighted allumer

light; lightly léger ; légèrement

lighter briquet

like aimer

like (adv.) comme

likely vraisemblable

likeness ressemblance

lip lèvre

lit (cf. light)

live vivre, habiter

living (for a) pour gagner sa vie

lock, lock up fermer à clef, enfermer

loll se prélasser

look avoir l'air

look (a) regard

look after surveiller

look like ressembler à

loom up apparaître, surgir

loop boucle ; passant *(vêtement)*

loosen, loosen up se relâcher, se décontracter

lose, lost, lost perdre

loser perdant

lot of (a) beaucoup de

loud fort, intense *(son)*

loudspeaker haut-parleur

lounge se prélasser

lounge (the) salon

lousy infect, moche

lovely joli, beau

loving; lovingly aimant ; amoureusement

low; lower bas ; inférieur

lower (a)baisser

lucky chanceux

luggage (invariable) bagages

lump masse

lung poumon

lying (cf. lie)

— M —

made of fait de, fabriqué en

madly follement

maid servante

mail (Am.); mail (the) poster ; courrier

main principal

make marque de fabrique

make out (made, made) distinguer

make sure (made, made) s'assurer de

make up; make up for compléter ; rattraper

make, made, made faire, fabriquer

maker fabricant

marshland marécage

mash écraser

match allumette

match an offer offrir autant que

matter sujet

matter (it doesn't) cela n'a pas d'importance

matter? (what's the) que se passe-t-il ?

maybe peut-être

meal repas

mean (adj.) vache, chameau, méchant

mean, meant, meant vouloir dire, signifier

meaning signification

means (by no) pas du tout

meat; meaty viande ; bien en chair

meekly humblement

meet, met, met (se) rencontrer

meeting rassemblement

mere simple

mess mess, cantine *(Militaire)*

met (cf. meet)

midday midi

middle milieu

midnight minuit

milk lait

mind esprit

mind (I don't) je m'en fiche

mind you! remarquez !

mine le(s) mien(s), la mienne, etc.

mingle with se mélanger à

miserable lamentable

miss; missing rater ; manquant, absent

mist brume

mistaken (be) se tromper

month; monthly mois ; mensuel

mood atmosphère ; humeur

more and more de plus en plus

morsel petit bout, bouchée

most la plupart, la plus grande partie

mostly principalement

motionless immobile

motor-cycle moto

mouth; mouthful bouche ; bouchée

move bouger

move (a) mouvement

moved ému

muck purée de pois

mud; muddy boue ; boueux

mug (sl.) andouille, imbécile

mum (keep) rester bouche cousue

myself moi-même

— N —

narrow; narrow (adj.) rétrécir ; étroit

nasty mesquin, mauvais

nasty mess (a) un sacré pétrin, de beaux draps

naughty osé, peu sage

near; nearly près, proche ; presque

neck cou

neither... nor ni... ni

nestle nicher

never jamais

new neuf, nouveau

news (pl.) nouvelle

newspaper journal

next suivant

nice joli

nick (sl.) piquer, faucher

night nuit

nightmare cauchemar

nobody, no one personne

nod faire un signe de tête

noise bruit

nonsense (invariable) sottises

noon midi

nose nez

nosey-parker curieux, fouineur

nostril narine

note billet de banque

notebook carnet de notes

nothing rien

notice remarquer

notice (a) avis

nowadays ces temps-ci, de nos jours

nowhere nulle part

nuisance fléau, calamité

number-plate plaque minéralogique

— O —

obviously visiblement

occur venir à l'esprit

odd étrange

off balance décontenancé

offence infraction

offer proposition

oily mielleux, onctueux

old vieux

old-fashioned démodé

once autrefois ; une fois

once (at) immédiatement

only seul, seulement

oozing émanation

openly ouvertement

operate *(faire)* marcher, fonctionner

order commander

order to (in) de façon à

otherwise autrement

ought to devoir

out of sight hors de vue

output production

outside à l'extérieur

outstretched étendu, déployé

over au-dessus, par-dessus

over (adj.) terminé

overcoat pardessus

overhear surprendre des paroles

overshaved trop bien rasé

own propre *(à soi)*

own; owner posséder; propriétaire

— P —

pace pas

pain douleur

paint; painting peinture; tableau

pal (fam.) copain, pote

palm paume de la main

panelling lambris, boiseries

pantry garde-manger

party (pl. parties) fête, réception

patch tache

pay, paid, paid payer

pebble galet

peculiar particulier, spécial

peek coup d'œil furtif

peer scruter

pencil crayon

pepper poivre

perform; performance exécuter; numéro, prestation

perhaps peut-être

pick one's nose se mettre les doigts dans le nez

pick up ramasser

picture imaginer, se représenter

picture (a) photo

piece morceau

pink rose

pith vigueur

pity (it's a) c'est dommage

plain simple

pain clothes (in) en civil

plane avion

plate assiette

play; player jouer; joueur

pleased content, satisfait

pleasure satisfaction

plot intrigue

poached poché

pocket poche

poised en équilibre

poke (one's head) passer *(la tête)*
pond mare
ponder méditer sur
pool enchères
poor pauvre
pop fourrer
pop up surgir
port bâbord
porthole hublot
positive (be) être certain
postponed retardé
pounce foncer sur
pound livre sterling
pour out verser *(liquide)*
power; powerful puissance ; puissant
pray prier
press; press together appuyer ; serrer
pretty joli
pretty (adv.) plutôt, assez
prevent empêcher
previous précédent
prickle picoter
pride fierté
prim guindé
primrose primevère
privacy intimité
prop-stand béquille
propeller hélice
properly correctement
proud; proudly fier ; fièrement

provided that pourvu que, à condition que
publisher éditeur
pudding dessert
puffy gonflé
pull tirer
pull (a) poignée, cordon
pull (oneself) up se hisser
pull away enlever
pull in s'arrêter *(véhicule)*
pull up remonter
purposeful résolu
purposely volontairement
purr ronronner
purse (Am.) sac à main
purser commissaire de bord
push pousser
put up (put, put) proposer
put, put, put mettre

— Q —

queer étrange, bizarre
quick(ly) rapide*(ment)*
quiet(ly) silencieux ; silencieusement
quite tout à fait

rabbit lapin

race, race track course, champ de courses

racket escroquerie

radiance éclat, rayonnement

rail bastingage

rain pluie

raise lever, élever

ran (cf. run)

rang (cf. ring)

range échelle

range (within) à portée de tir

rate (at any) en tout cas

rather; I'd rather plutôt; je préférerais

reach; reach for atteindre; chercher à atteindre

read, read, read lire

ready prêt

real vrai

recall se rappeler

reckless imprudent

recognize reconnaître

record enregistrer

reflect refléter

relieved soulagé

relish délectation

remain rester

remainder reste

remember se souvenir

remind rappeler

remove enlever

repair réparer

reply; reply (a) répondre; réponse

repulsive répugnant

rescue sauver, secourir

rest poser, appuyer; se reposer

restful reposant

resume reprendre

retain retenir

retainer serviteur

retreat reculer

reverse marche arrière

rid of (get) se débarrasser de

ride, rode, ridden chevaucher

rifleman fusilier

right droite

right (adv.) tout droit; complètement

right (be) avoir raison

right (that's) c'est exact

right (the) le droit

right away immédiatement

right-angle angle droit

rightly justement

rim bord

ring bague

ring, rang, rung sonner

ripcord poignée d'ouverture *(parachute)*

rise, rose, risen s'élever

road route

roar vrombir

roast rôtir

roll rouler

roll (the) roulis *(Naut)* ; vol en tonneau *(Aviat.)*

roll off dégringoler

roof toit

rotten pourri

rough agité *(mer)*

roundabout rond-point

row rangée

rubber gomme, caoutchouc

rudder-bar palonnier *(Aviat.)*

rug couverture, plaid

run distance parcourue

run, ran, run courir, faire courir

rush se précipiter

rusty rouillé

— S —

sad triste

saddle selle

safe sûr, en sécurité

safety sécurité

sag s'affaisser

sagging pendant

said (cf. say)

sail faire du bateau *(à voile)*

sailor marin

salt; salt-cellar sel ; salière

same; the same semblable ; le ou la même

sank (cf. sink)

sat (cf. sit)

satisfied convaincu

savings (pl.) économies

saw (cf. see)

say, said, said dire

scared (be) être effrayé

scarf écharpe

scent senteur, odeur

schoolboy écolier

scream; scream (a) hurler ; cri perçant

screw up plisser *(les yeux)*

sea mer

search fouiller, faire des recherches

seasoned expérimenté

seat siège ; dossier *(chaise)*

seated assis

see, saw, seen voir

seek, sought, sought chercher

seem sembler

207

seldom rarement

self-preservation instinct de conservation

sell, sold, sold vendre

send, sent, sent envoyer

serious grave

set (T.V.) poste de télévision

set, set, set placer, situer, mettre

settle s'installer, se fixer

several plusieurs

shadow ombre

shake, shook, shaken secouer

shape forme

shark requin

sharply brusquement, sèchement

sheet drap

shift bouger

ship bateau, navire

shirt chemise

shiver trembler

shoelace lacet de chaussure

shook (cf. shake)

shoot out (shot, shot) sortir

shoot, shot, shot tirer, tuer qqn avec une arme

shot (a) tir

shoulder épaule

shout; shout (a) crier ; cri

show montrer, laisser voir

shrewdness perspicacité

shrill aigu

shrug hausser les épaules

shut, shut, shut fermer

shy, shyly timide, timidement

side côté, paroi *(falaise)*

sideboard buffet

sideways, sidewise de côté

sight; in sight vue, vision ; en vue

silk, silky soie, soyeux

sill (window) rebord de la fenêtre

silly idiot

silt up s'ensabler, s'envaser

silver; silversmith argent ; orfèvre

since depuis

single seul, unique

sink, sank, sunk couler

sip boire une gorgée

sit, sat, sat s'asseoir, être assis

skill qualification

skin peau

skinny maigre

skintight ajusté, collant *(vêtement)*

skip sautiller

sky ciel

slack off relâcher

slacken réduire

sleep, slept, slept dormir

sleeve manche *(vêtement)*

slice tranche

slide, slid, slid glisser

slight, slightly léger, légèrement

slim mince

slip glisser

sloping tombant

slow down ralentir

slow, slowly lent, lentement

sly; slyly rusé, malin ; avec espièglerie

smack one's lips se lécher les babines

small petit

smell, smelt, smelt sentir

smile sourire

smoke, smoke (the) fumer, fumée

smooth lisse

smouldering fumant *(de colère)*

smug sûr de soi

snap parler d'un ton sec

snif humer

snip off couper

snort grogner

snow neige

so long as dans la mesure où

so on and so forth et ainsi de suite

soft, softly doux, doucement

soil terre

sold (cf. sell)

solicitor avocat

something quelque chose

sometimes quelquefois

somewhat quelque peu

somewhere quelque part

soon bientôt ; tôt, vite

sooner or later tôt ou tard

sorry désolé

sought (cf. seek)

sound reason bonne raison

sour aigre

spare en trop

spark étincelle

sparkle scintiller

sparrow moineau

speak, spoke, spoken parler

speck point, tache

spectacles (pl.) lunettes

speed, speed limit vitesse, limitation de vitesse

spell courte période

spell, spelt, spelt or spelled épeler

spend, spent, spent passer *(temps)* ; dépenser *(argent)*

spill renverser

spinster vieille fille

spit, spat, spat cracher

spite of (in) en dépit de

splash patauger

splinter *(se)* fendre

split se fendre

spoke (cf. speak)

spot apercevoir

spot (a) endroit ; tache

spout bec verseur

sprang (cf. spring)

spray écume

spread, spread, spread s'étendre

spreadeagled bras et jambes écartés

spring, sprang, sprung bondir

sprinkle asperger

spurt jet

squeeze presser

squirrel écureuil

stagger tituber

stake enjeu

stalk traquer

stand, stood, stood être *(se tenir)* debout

stare at regarder fixement

start up sursauter

start ; starter démarrer ; démarreur

state état

station gare

station (police) commissariat de police

stay rester, séjourner

steady oneself se mettre d'aplomb

steam ; steam (the) fumer ; vapeur

steep abrupt, escarpé

step marche ; pas

step out sortir

stick out (stuck, stuck) ressortir

stick, stuck, stuck coller

stiff raide

still (adj.); still (adv.) immobile ; toujours, encore

sting, stung, stung piquer

stood (cf. stand)

storey (Am.) étage

story histoire

straight *(tout)* droit

strain s'efforcer de

stranger étranger

strap ; strap (a) attacher ; sangle

stream filet ; ruisseau

street rue

stroll marcher nonchalamment

strong fort
struggle se battre
stubby gros et court
stuck (cf. stick) coincé
study; study (a) étudier ;
  bureau
stung (cf. sting)
subside baisser
such tel
suck; suck (a) sucer ;
  bouffée (cigarette)
suffer souffrir
suitcase valise
summer été
summons assignation à
  comparaître
sun-roof toit ouvrant
  (Auto)
sunk (cf. sink)
sunny ensoleillé
supercilious hautain
surgeon chirurgien
suspicious méfiant
swallow avaler
swear, swore, sworn jurer
sweat sueur
sweet doux
swerve faire un écart
swiftly rapidement
swim, swam, swum nager
swing, swung, swung ba-
  lancer, lancer
swirl tourner (en spirale)

switch on; switch off allumer ; éteindre
swung (cf. swing)

— T —

tablecloth nappe
tail queue
take off (took, taken) enlever
take, took, taken prendre,
  emmener
tale conte, récit
talk to parler à
tall grand, haut
tangle embrouiller
taper aller en diminuant
taste; taste (the) goûter ;
  goût
taster goûteur
tear larme
tear, tore, torn déchirer
tease taquiner
teeth (cf. tooth)
tell, told, told dire, racon-
  ter
tense tendu
terrific fantastique
Thank God! Dieu merci !
thick épais
thicken épaissir
thigh cuisse

thimbleful doigt ou goutte de liquide

thin; thinness mince; minceur

think, thought, thought penser

third troisième

thoroughly à fond

thought idée, pensée

thoughtful attentionné; pensif

thoughfully pensivement

thousand (a or one) mille

thread one's way se frayer un chemin

throat gorge

through par, à travers

throw, threw, thrown jeter

thumb pouce *(doigt)*

thumb a lift lever le pouce (auto-stop)

ticket contravention, P.V.

tidy packet (a) un bon paquet, une sacrée somme

tight serré, tendu

tighten serrer

till jusqu'à ce que

tin boîte de fer blanc

tinkle résonner

tiny minuscule

tip bout, extrémité; pourboire

tip verser; donner un pourboire

tired fatigué

tired of (be) en avoir assez de

titchy (sl.) petit

together ensemble

told (cf. tell)

tongue langue

tonight ce soir

too aussi

took (cf. take)

tooth (pl. teeth) dent

top hat chapeau haut-de-forme

top; top (the) supérieur; sommet, haut

tore (cf. tear)

toughness dureté

towards vers

town ville

toy jouet

tracer balle traçante

trade profession

trainer entraîneur

tramp vagabond

travel; traveller voyager; voyageur

tray plateau

tread, trod, trodden or trod marcher avec précaution

tremendous; tremen-

dously énorme ; extrê-
mement

trick tour, truc

trickle down s'écouler

trifle (a) un rien

trigger; trigger button gâchette ; bouton de tir

trip voyage

trouble (take) prendre la
peine de

trouble; be in trouble problème ; avoir des en-
nuis

trousers pantalon

truck (Am.) camion

true vrai

trust faire confiance à

trusting confiant

try essayer

turn (it's your) c'est ton
tour

turn away; turn back se
détourner ; se retour-
ner

turn over retourner

twerp (sl.) idiot, andouille, crétin

twice deux fois

twist tordre

twitch avoir un tic

— U —

ugly horrible

unable incapable

unbutton déboutonner

unconcerned indifférent

under sous, au-dessous

**understand, understood,
understood** compren-
dre

undo défaire

uneasiness malaise

unemployed (be) être sans
travail

unexpected inattendu

unknown inconnu

unless à moins que

unlucky malchanceux

unmistakably sans aucun
doute

unruffled imperturbable

until jusqu'à *(ce que)*

unusual inhabituel, peu
commun

up and down de haut en
bas

upright droit

upstairs en haut, à l'étage

upstretched relevé

urge presser

urgently avec insistance

use utiliser

usual(ly) habituel*(lement)*

— V —

vacant libre
vegetable légume
venture risquer
vineyard vignoble
vintage millésime (vin)

— W —

wages salaire, gages
wait for; waiting (the) attendre ; attente
wake sillage
Wales Pays de Galles
walk marcher
wander errer
want vouloir
war guerre
warm tiède
warn; warning avertir ; avertissement
wash laver
watch out for faire attention à, se méfier de
watch, watch for observer, guetter
watch; watchmaker montre ; horloger
wave faire signe de la main ; agiter

wave (a) vague
way manière, façon ; chemin, route
weakness faiblesse
wear, wore, worn porter (sur soi)
weather temps
wedge enfoncer
week semaine
weight poids
well up monter, s'amplifier
wet mouillé, trempé
wheel (steering-) volant
wheelbase empattement (Auto)
whenever chaque fois que
while pendant que
while (a) moment
whisper chuchoter
whitebait petits poissons frits
whiteness blancheur
whole entier
whopping (fam.) énorme
wicker osier
wide large
wife femme (épouse)
willing volontaire, consentant
win, won, won gagner
wind vent
window vitre (voiture)
windshield pare-brise

214

wine vin
wing aile
wink clin d'œil
winner gagnant
wish souhaiter, désirer
wisp brin
wistful mélancolique
withdraw, withdrew, withdrawn *(se)* retirer
within à l'intérieur de ; en l'espace de
without sans
witness témoin
won (cf. win)
wonder; wonder (the) se demander ; étonnement
wonderful merveilleux
wood; wooden bois ; en bois
word; my word! mot, parole ; ma parole !
wore (cf. wear)
work faire fonctionner
world monde
worry *(s')*inquiéter
worse; get worse pire ; empirer
worth (be) valoir la peine
wounded blessé
wrap up emballer

wrapped enveloppé
wrist poignet
write, wrote, written écrire
writer écrivain
wrong (be) avoir tort
wrong, get sb. wrong mal, comprendre qqn de travers
wrote (cf. write)

— Y —

yard mesure de longueur = 91,4 cm
year année
yearning aspiration
yell hurler
yellow jaune
yesterday hier
yet; not yet cependant ; pas encore
young jeune
yourself toi-même, vous-mêmes

— Z —

zoom se rapprocher

Composition réalisée par COMPOFAC – PARIS

Imprimé en France sur Presse Offset par

BRODARD & TAUPIN

GROUPE CPI

La Flèche (Sarthe).
N° d'imprimeur : 4126 – Dépôt légal Édit. 6548-09/2000
LIBRAIRIE GÉNÉRALE FRANÇAISE - 43, quai de Grenelle - 75015 Paris.
ISBN : 2 - 253 - 05029 - 6

Les Langues Modernes

Bilingue

Série anglaise dirigée par Pierre Nordon

Les ouvrages de la collection *Les Langues Modernes/Bilingue*
vous proposent sous une forme très claire :
▷ des textes d'écrivains étrangers de réputation internationale,
dans une palette de genres et de styles aussi variés que possible,
▷ une traduction fidèle et précise, sans être étroitement littérale,
▷ une introduction critique permettant d'approfondir le sens des
textes,
▷ de nombreuses notes de caractère culturel qui prolongent cette
introduction dans le détail, et des précisions linguistiques éclairant
certains tours de traduction.,
▷ l'enregistrement sur cassette de passages significatifs quant à la
phonétique.

La collection *Les Langues Modernes/Bilingue* entend permettre
ainsi au plus grand nombre une authentique compréhension des
littératures et par conséquent des cultures étrangères.

Déjà parus :
Joseph Conrad : *Heart of Darkness*
Katherine Mansfield : *The Bay and Other Short Stories*
R. L. Stevenson : *The Strange Case of Dr. Jekyll and Mr. Hyde*
Alan Sillitoe : *Revenge and Other Short Stories*
Erskine Caldwell : *Selected Short Stories*
XXX : *American Short Stories*

Les Langues Modernes

A. Sanford Wolf *et* Michèle Wolf

Speak American

Speak American est une *méthode moderne d'apprentissage* de la langue américaine qui s'adresse tout autant aux étudiants qu'aux stagiaires de la formation permanente qui souhaitent acquérir rapidement une bonne maîtrise de l'américain d'aujourd'hui.

Elle a pour objet de familiariser le lecteur avec les particularités de la langue et de lui permettre d'utiliser à bon escient divers registres d'emploi : familier, courant, argotique.

Chacun des douze chapitres s'inspire d'un fait divers authentique ou vraisemblable, et se présente successivement sous deux formes :

▷ vécu : c'est un dialogue vivant, *The Event* (intégralement enregistré sur cassette),

▷ raconté : c'est un extrait de presse, *The Newspaper Story*.

Ces textes sont complétés par des *Notes* sur les personnages, les noms propres et les lieux, de brèves notices d'information sur les journaux, ainsi que des remarques sur les américanismes *(People, Names and Places, Newspapers, Americanisms)*. Chaque chapitre est suivi d'exercices récapitulatifs *(Review Exercises)* et d'exercices enregistrés sur cassette *(Recorded Exercises)*. Les corrigés de ces exercices sont placés en fin de volume.